art
starts

101 art activites for the art classroom

art ideas developed and collected
by
Penny Kite Markowitz

Foreward

Art Starts contains over 100 activities that I have developed over twenty years of teaching art. These activities can be used as bellringers, as a review, or as exit slips. Some activities are for students that finish their art projects ahead of the class, some are sketchbook prompts and some are art appreciation/history research ideas. Most activities can be done in minutes at the start or end of a class and some may take up to an hour or more to complete.

Art Starts is divided into different sections including the elements of design, the principles of design, drawing, lettering, art appreciation, sketchbook prompts, early project finishers, and graphic organizers

Most pages have two mini tasks to be completed. I like giving these to the student in a half page format for several reasons. One, if it is a bell ringer or warm-up they know exactly what they are getting because they are the same size and color every day. My students know a warm-up is always on yellow paper. Also it is nice to run to the copier once every two days since two can be printed at a time. Finally, I give them a large envelope to keep all of their returned papers and putting a half sheet in a large 9 x 12 inch envelope is a breeze.

The sketchbook prompts and "What do I do when I finish?" assignments are also on half sheets but most of the art appreciation and art history are full sheets and may require some research on the part of the students. The section on graphic organizers is half sheets and everything in the book can be printed nicely on a letter size sheet of copy paper.

Some of these activities are drawing tasks that require copying a design or concept into a space directly below it. I think it is an excellent way for students to draw what they see. They are not only reviewing an element such as line, but they are also practicing their skills at seeing and duplicating what they see, this will lead to enhanced drawing skills. Some tasks ask students to take the information they have been given and develop ideas of their own. Most of the activities are rather open ended and may be used in a number of different ways.

Since teaching art utilizes a different approach than the other core subjects, I have had a difficult time finding suitable ideas to use with my students. So I decided to develop a collection of ideas that over the years evolved into Art Starts.

Penny Kite Markowitz

art
starts

elements of design

element of design - color

primary colors	secondary colors	tertiary colors	complementary colors

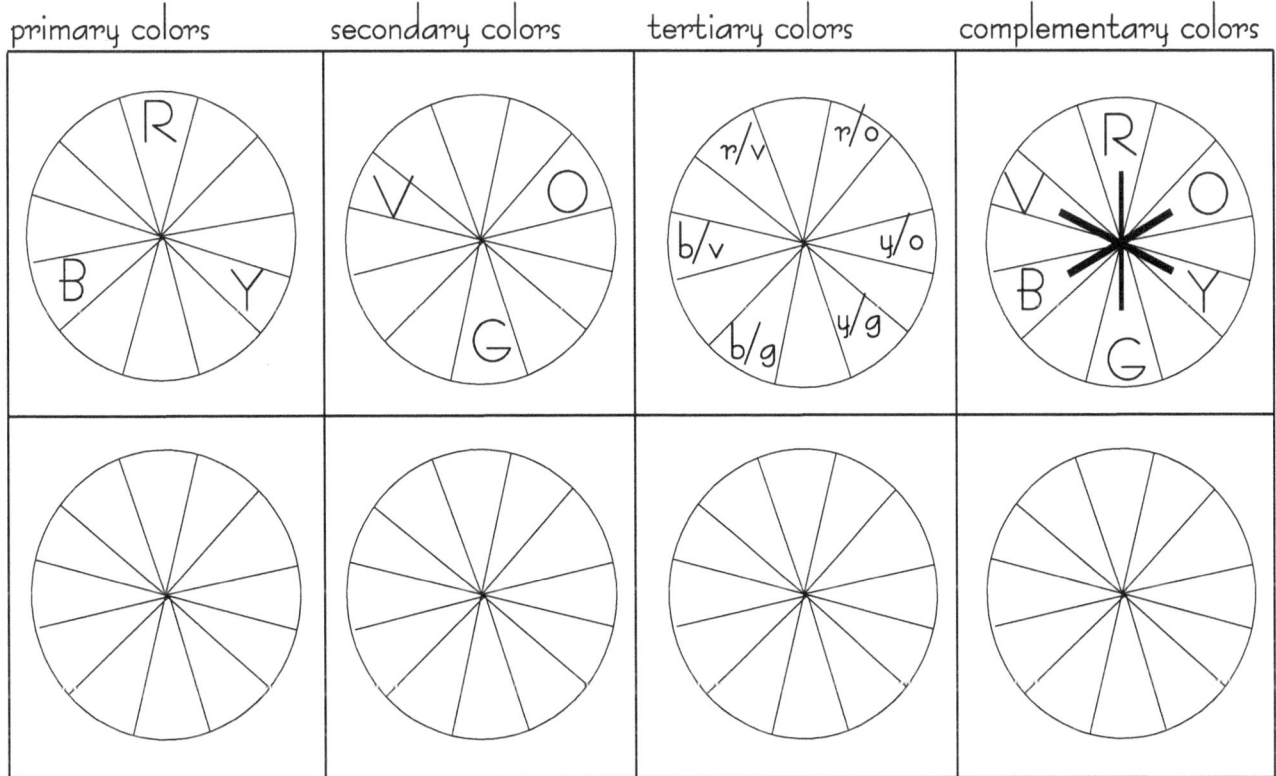

element of color - color schemes

warm	cool	monochromatic	analogous
yellow	blue	all shades and tints of one color	colors side by side on the color wheel
orange	green		
red	violet		

color swatches for color wheel

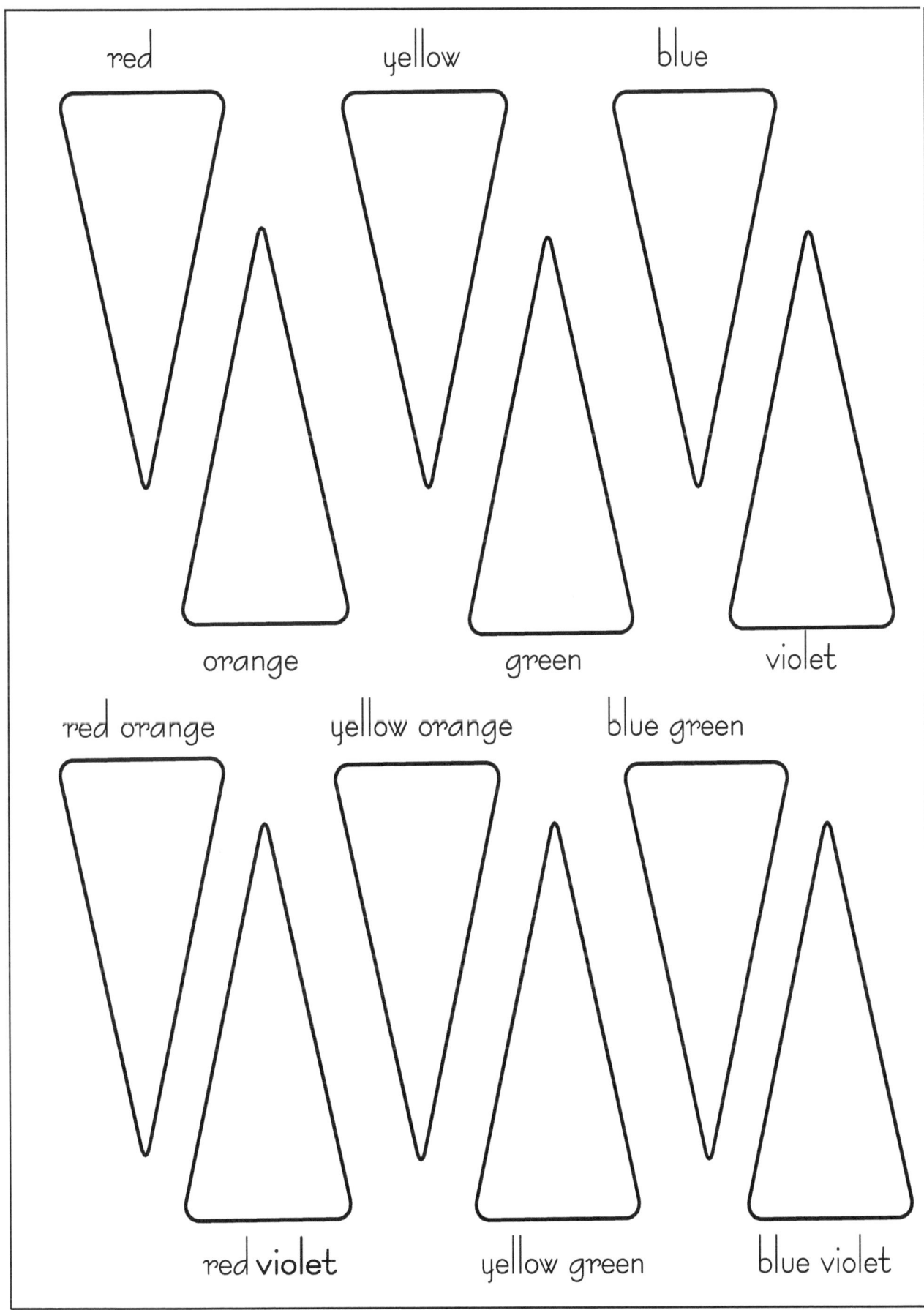

red

yellow

blue

orange

green

violet

red orange

yellow orange

blue green

red violet

yellow green

blue violet

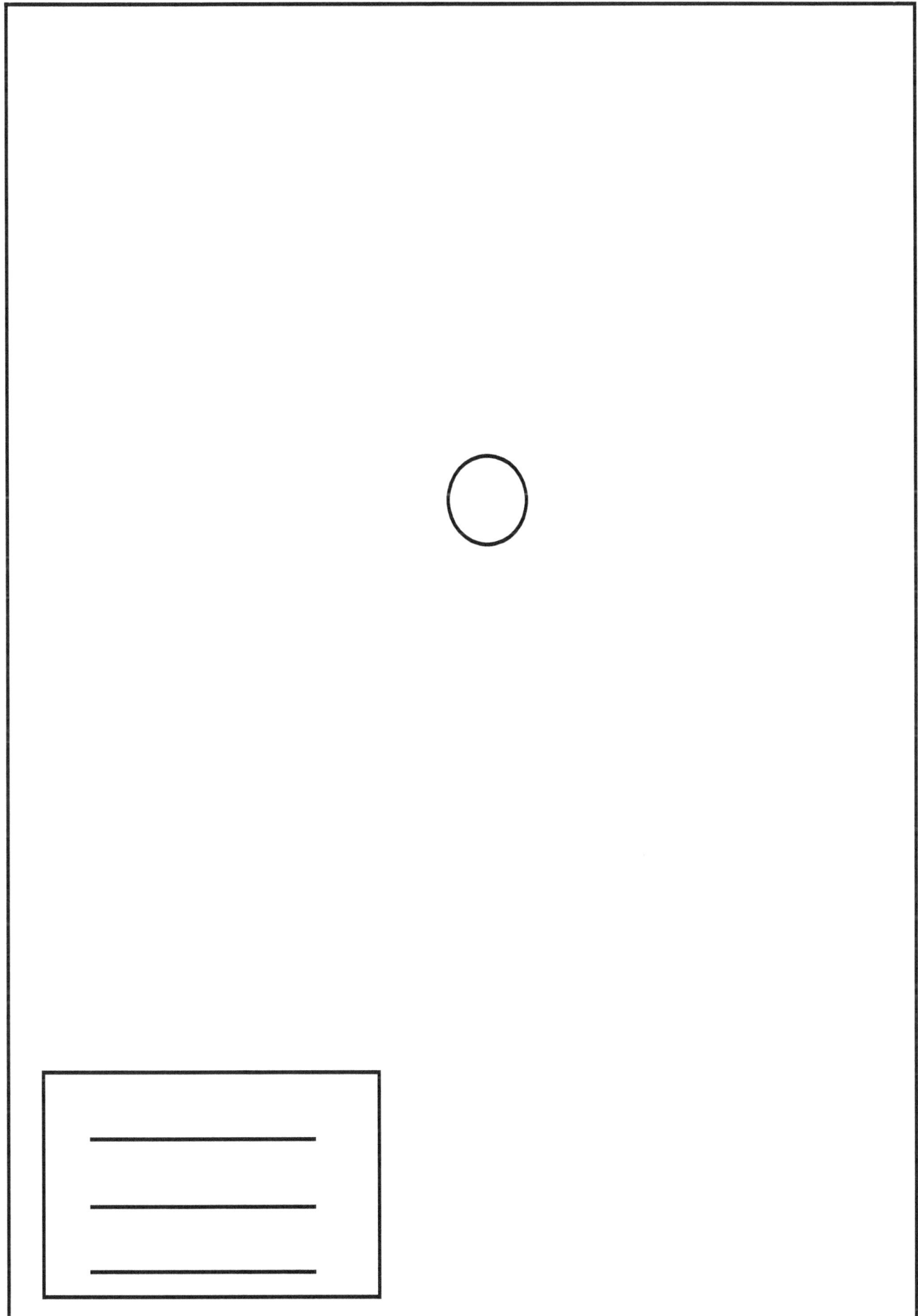

layout for finished color wheel

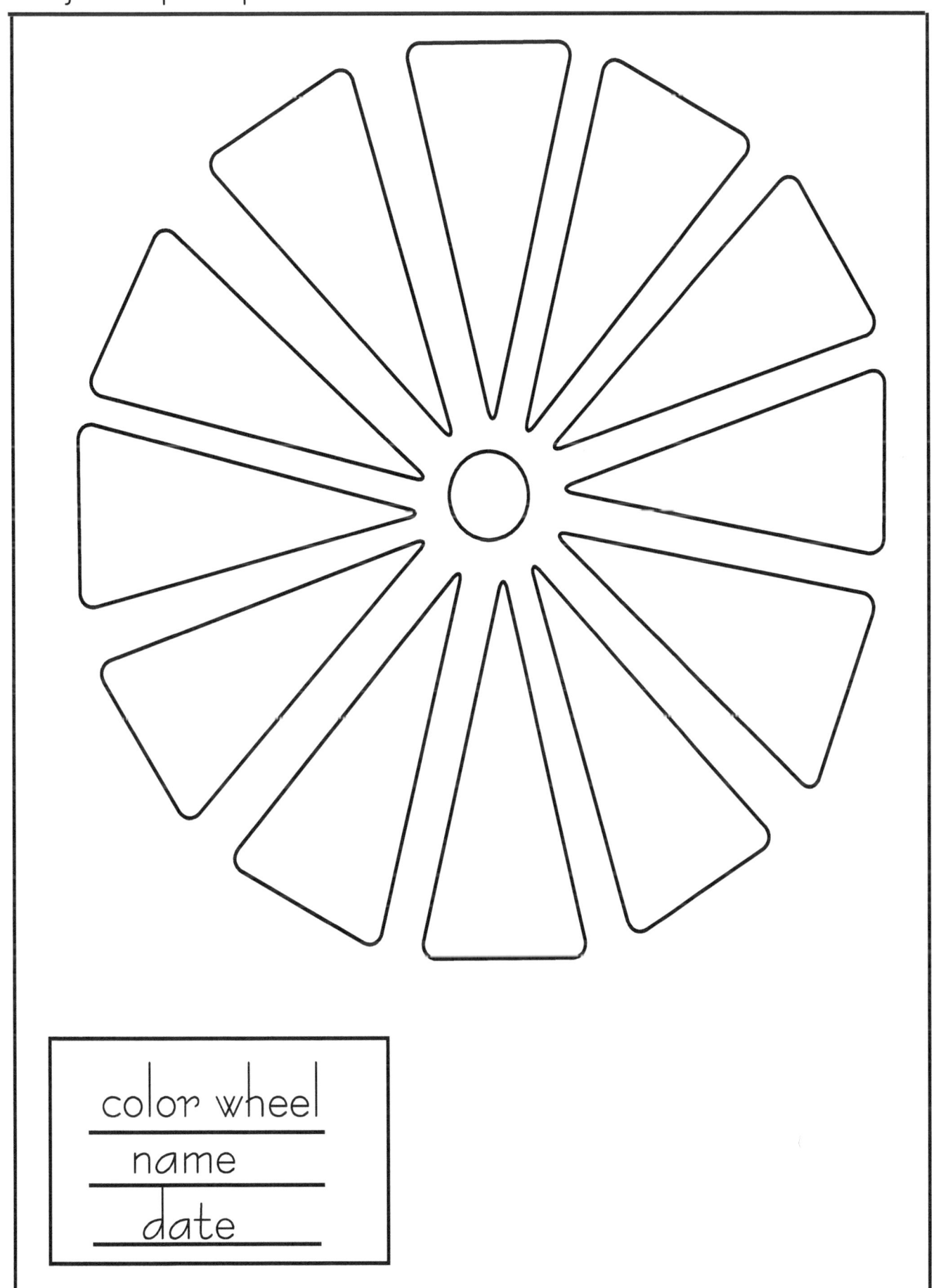

color wheel
name
date

color theory - color schemes

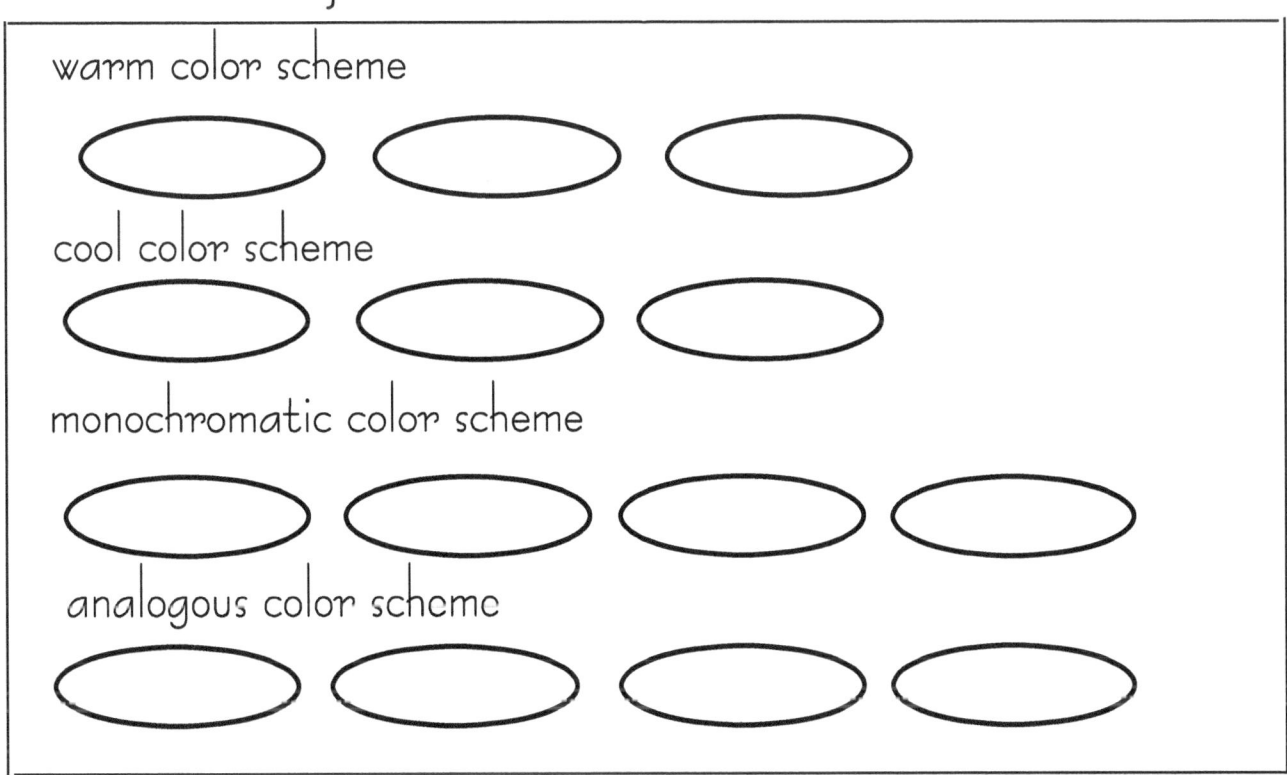

warm color scheme

cool color scheme

monochromatic color scheme

analogous color scheme

color theory - complementary color schemes

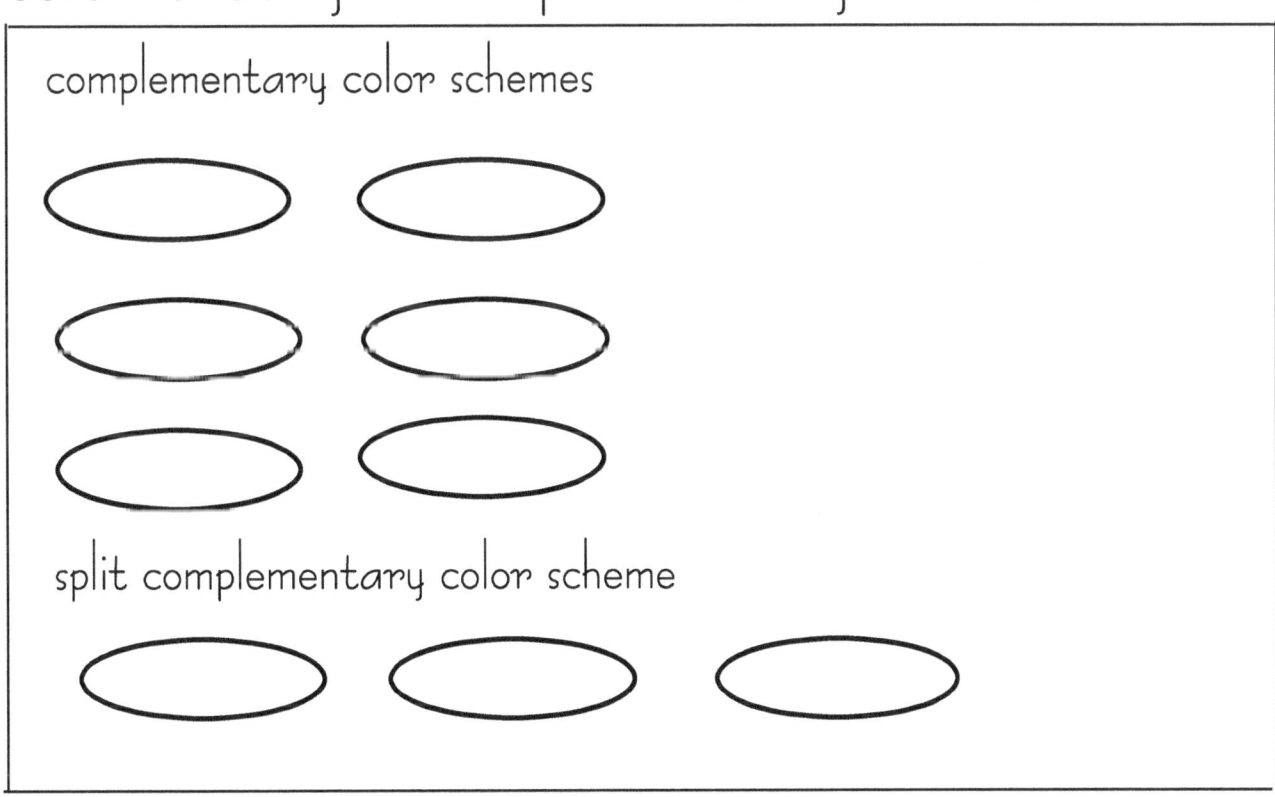

complementary color schemes

split complementary color scheme

element of design - line

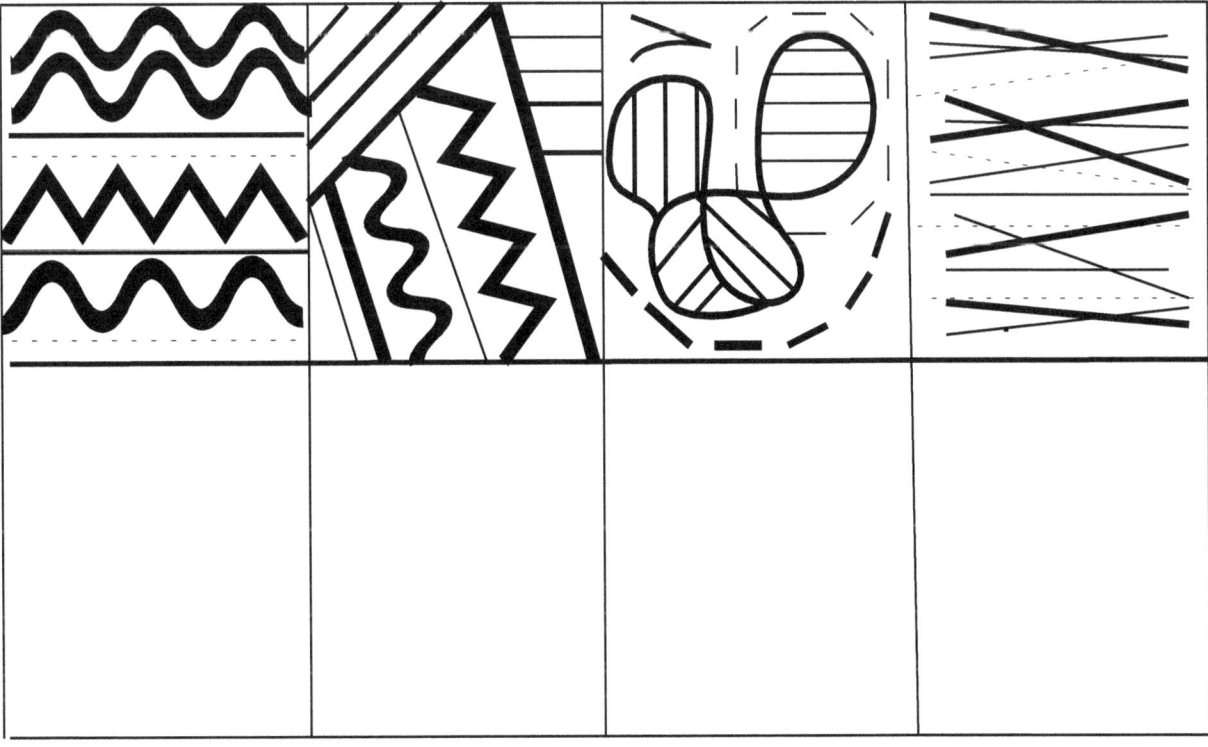

element of design - line
use lines to draw these designs or make four drawings of your own

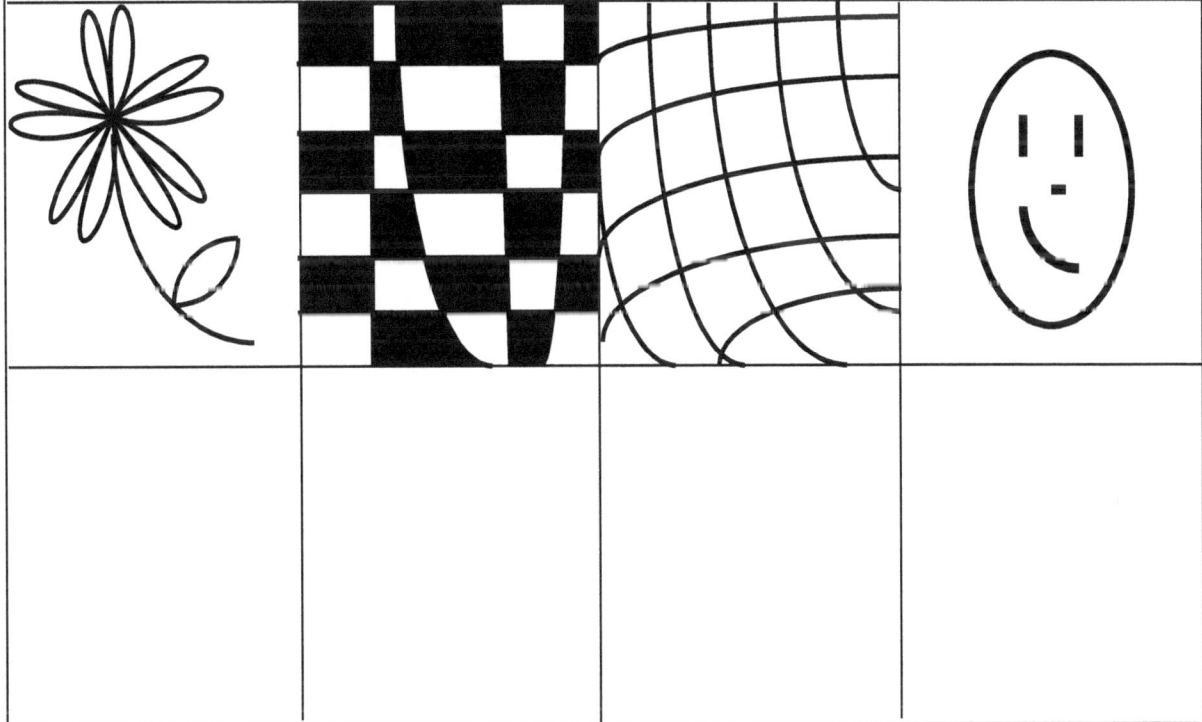

element of design - shape

geometric	free form	natural	mixed

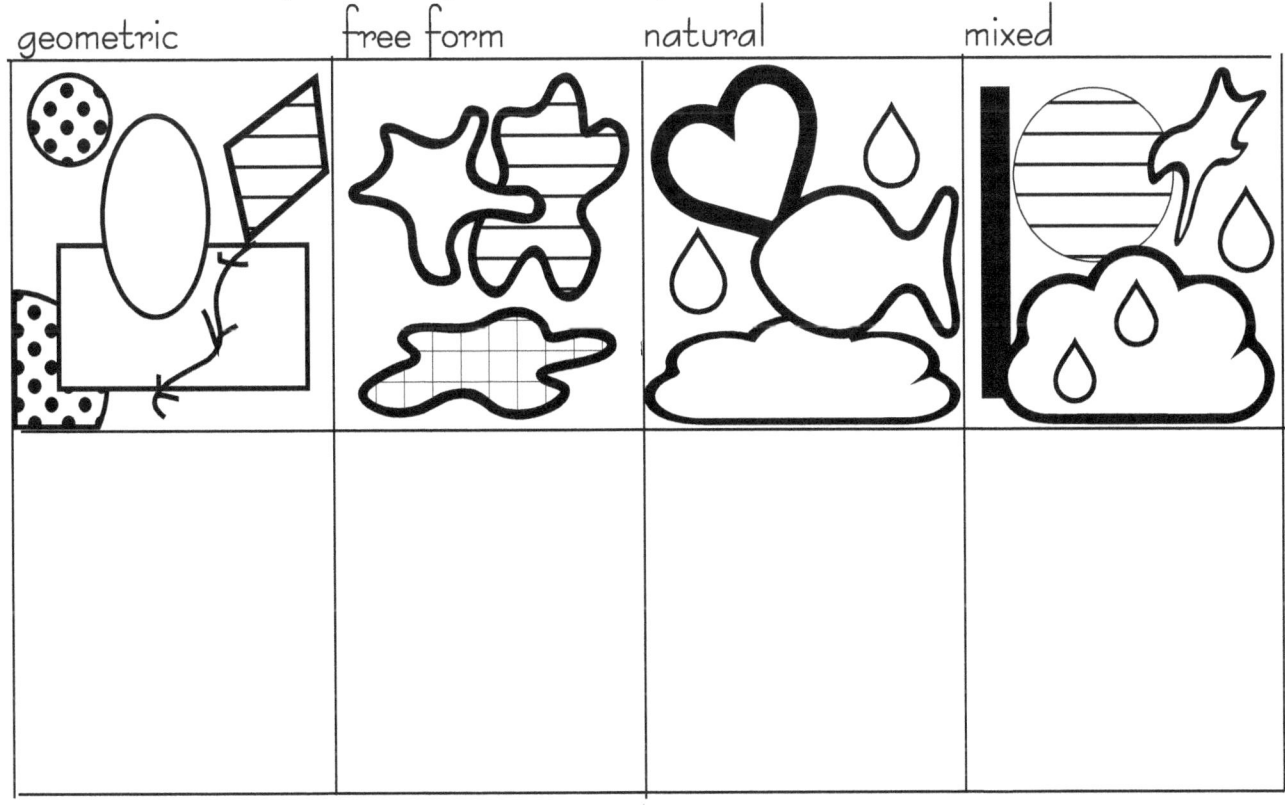

look for shapes to help you draw

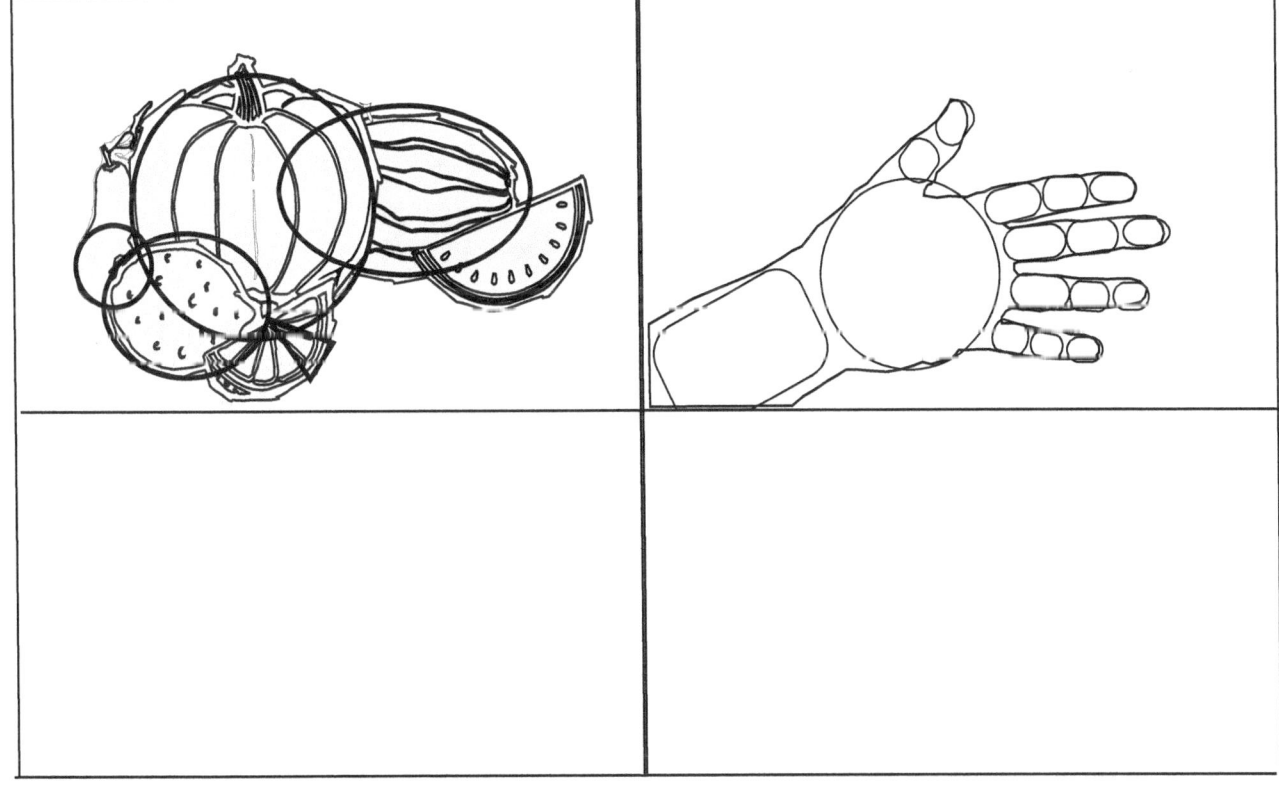

element of design - space

overlapping   perspective   positive/neg   object size

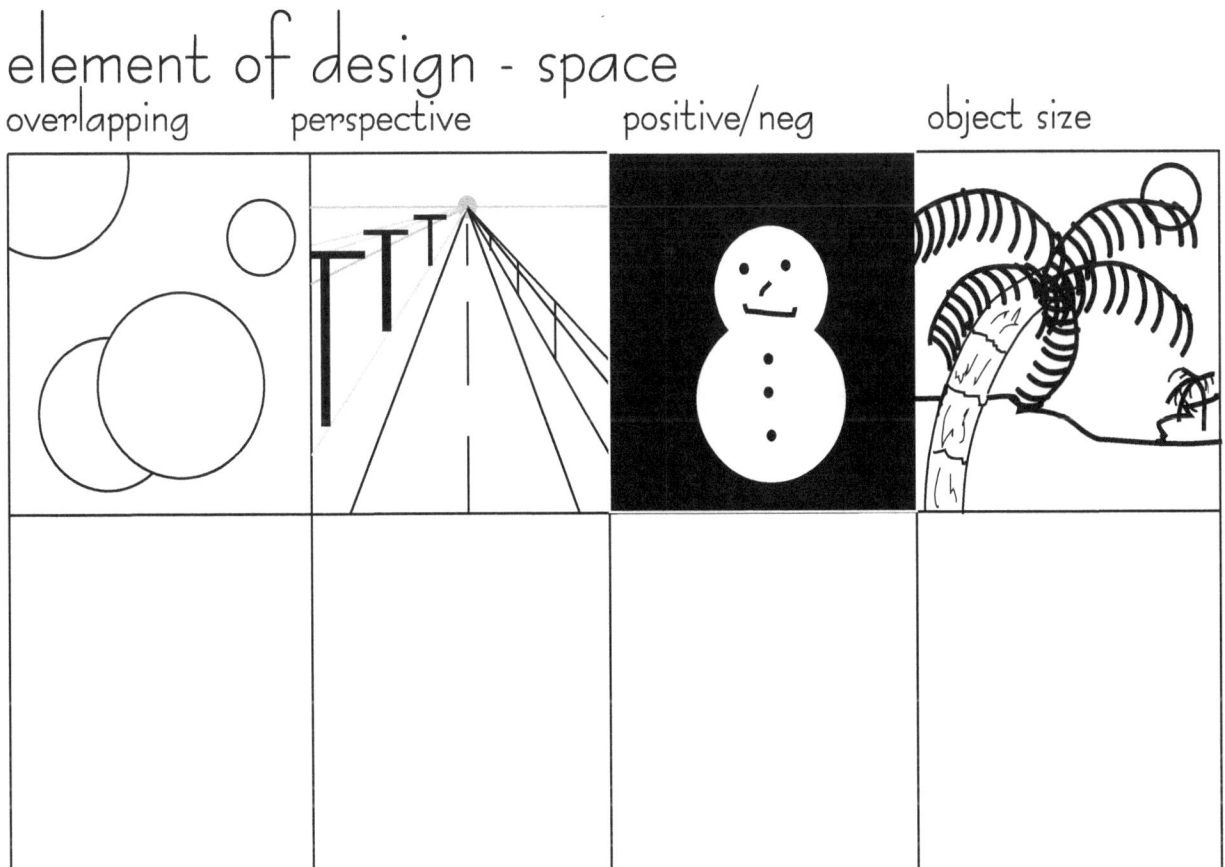

one-point perspective

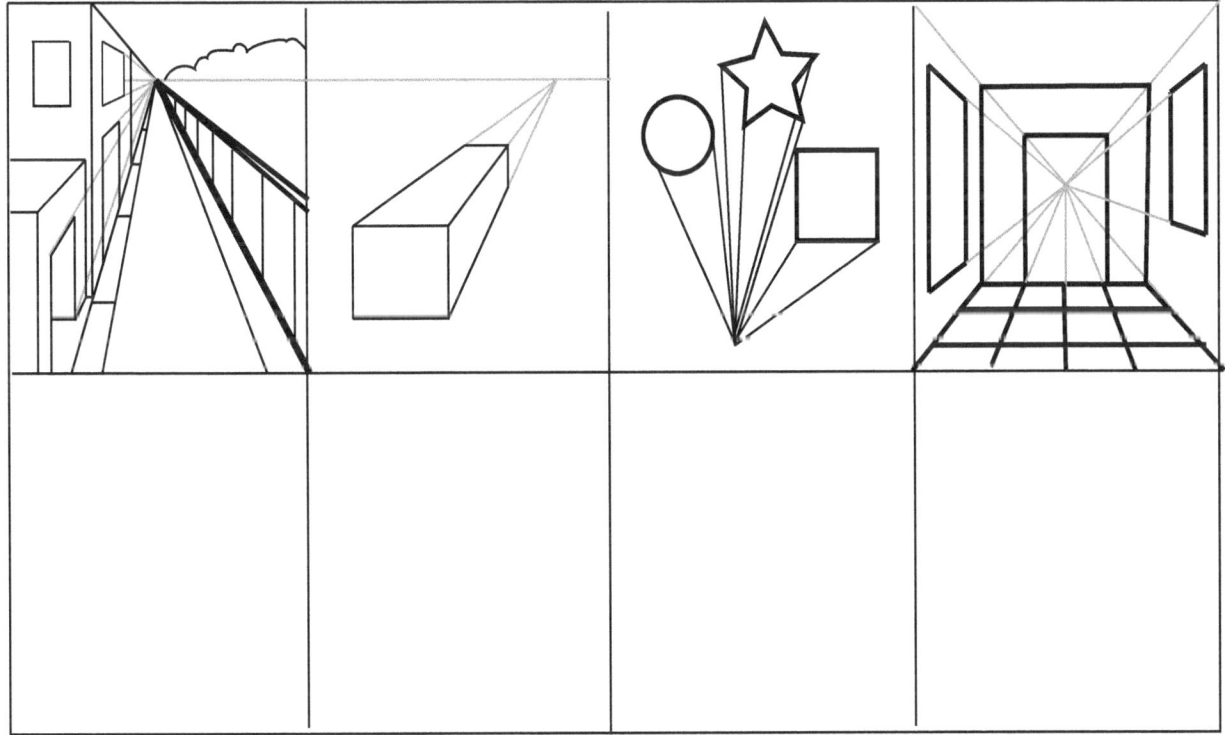

element of design - space
two-point perspective

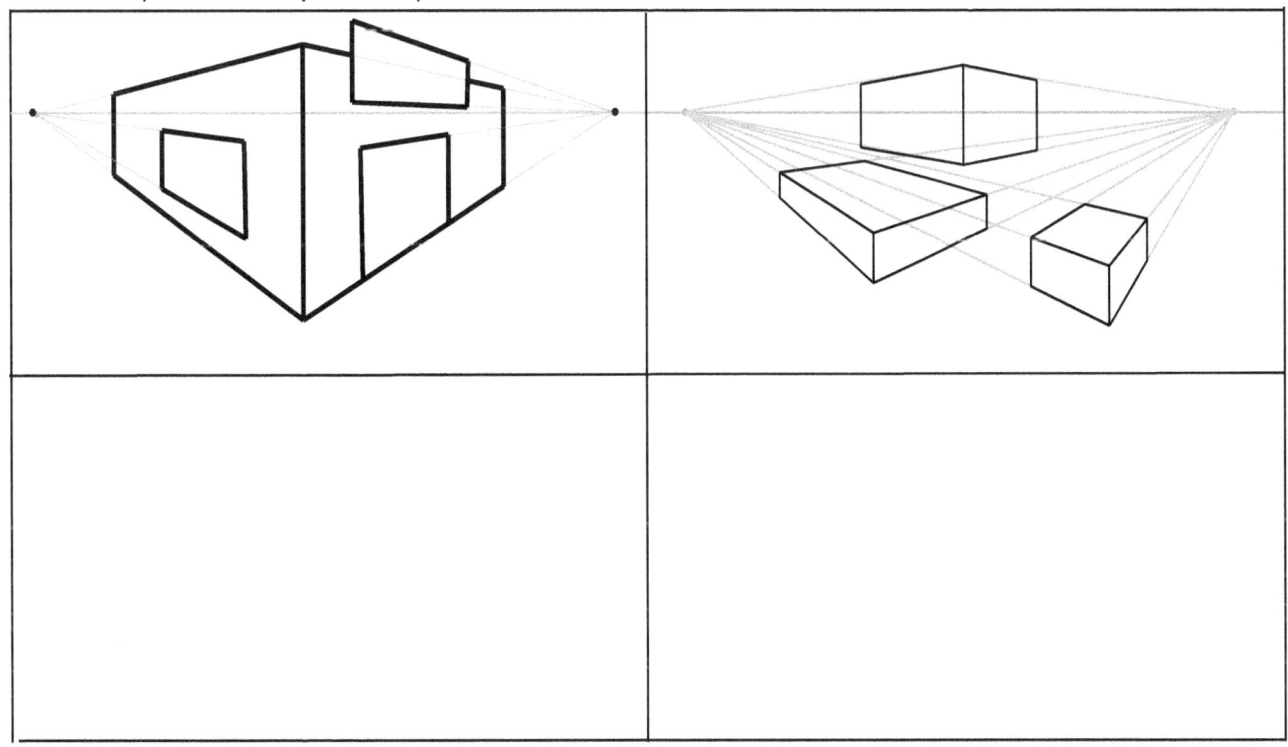

two-point perspective

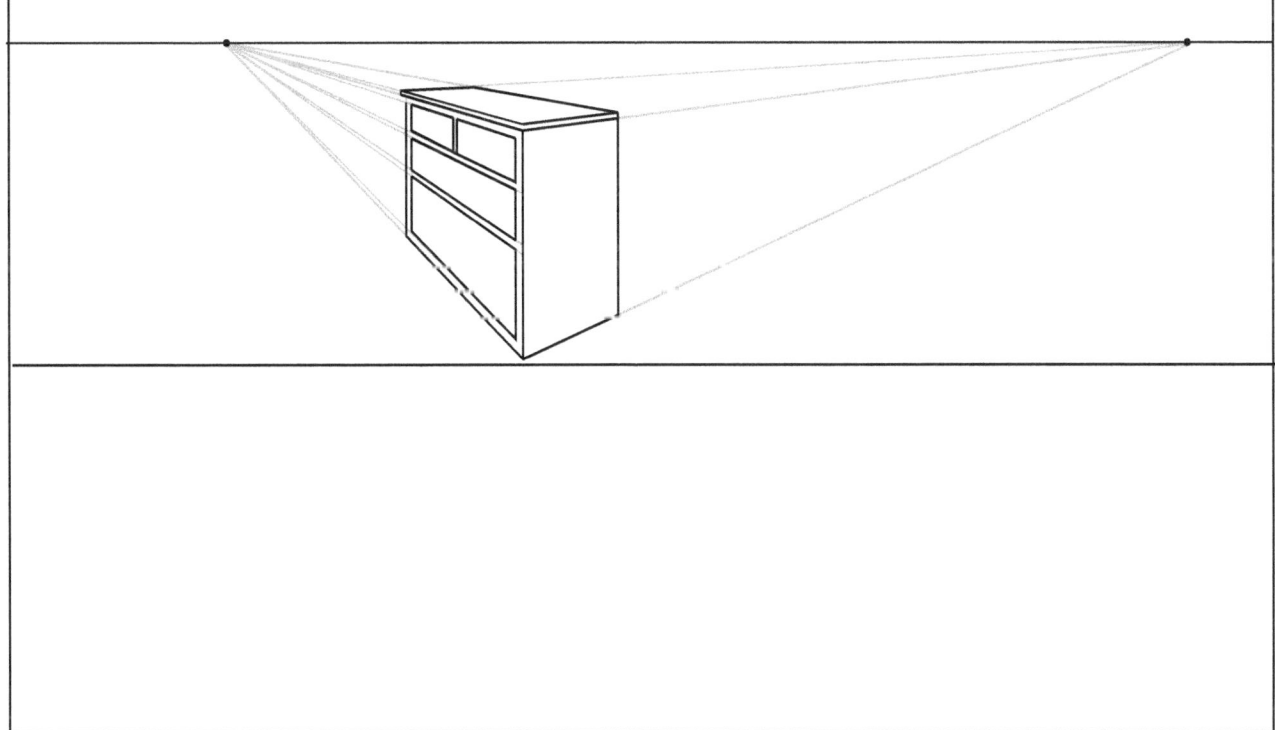

element of design - texture/implied texture

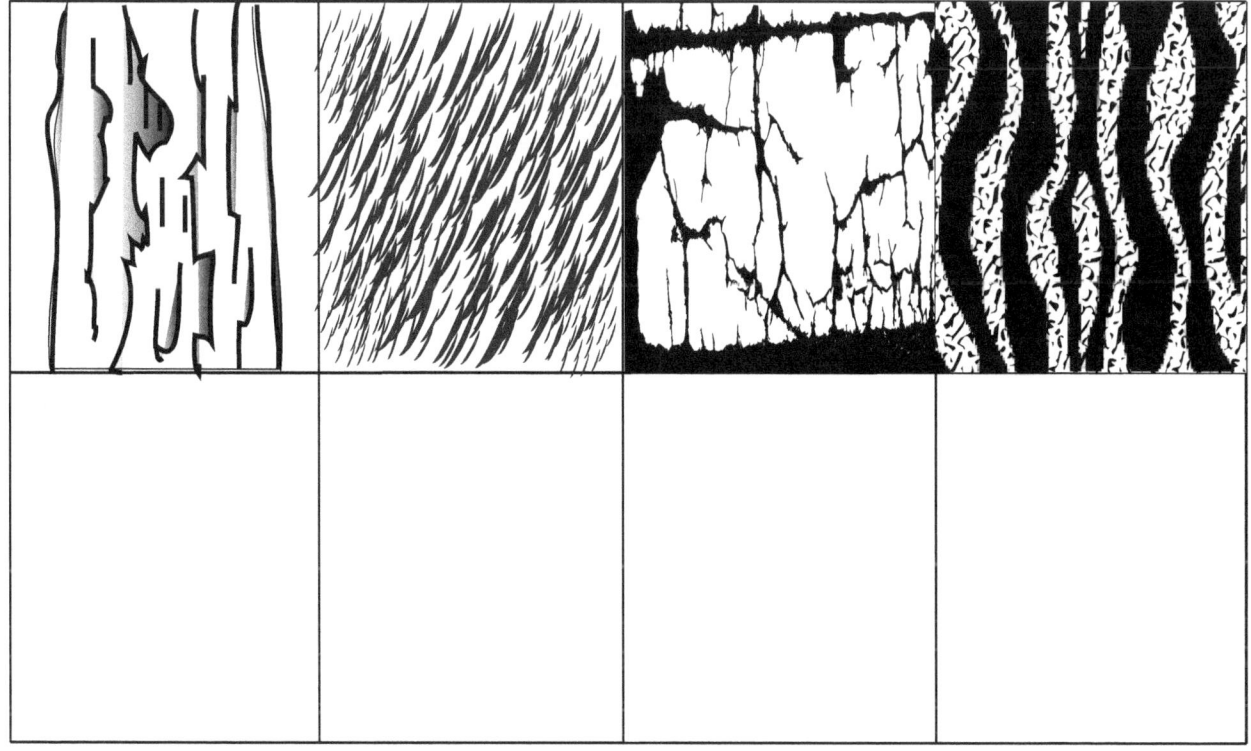

element of design - pattern textures

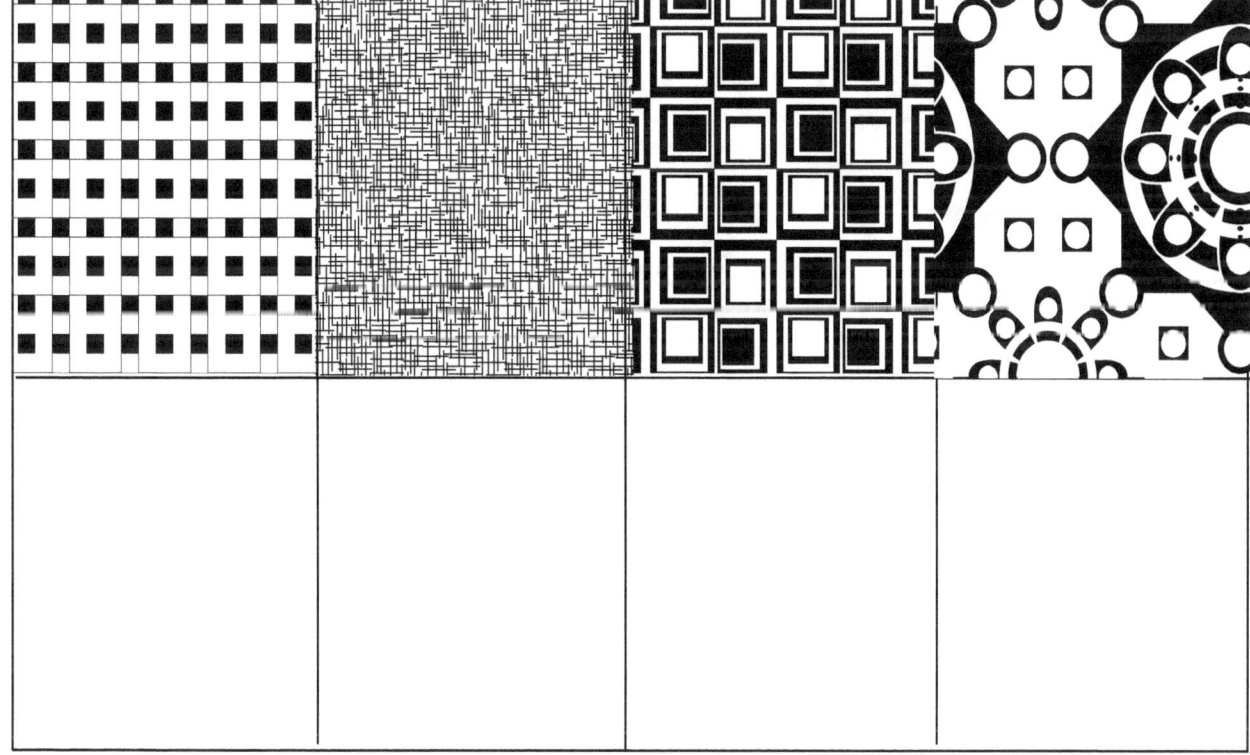

value with ink - lines

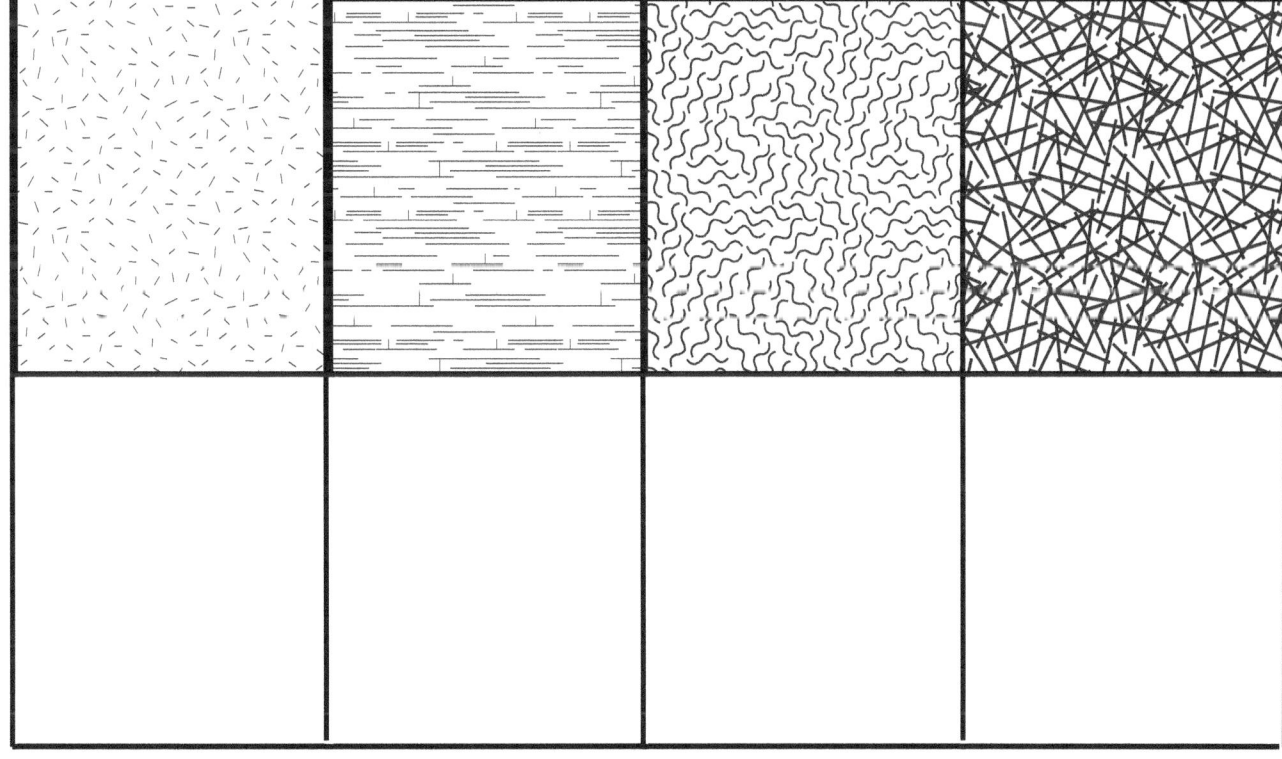

creating value with ink

value

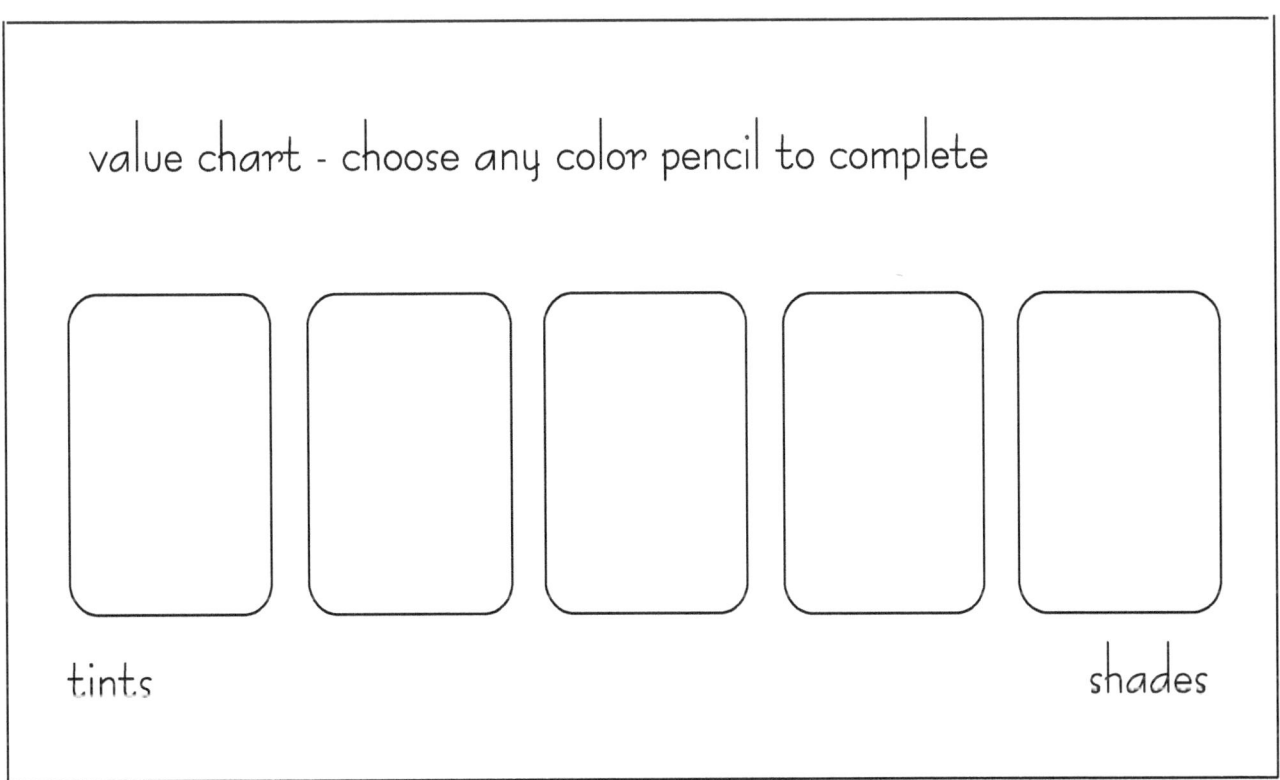

value chart - choose any color pencil to complete

tints   shades

value

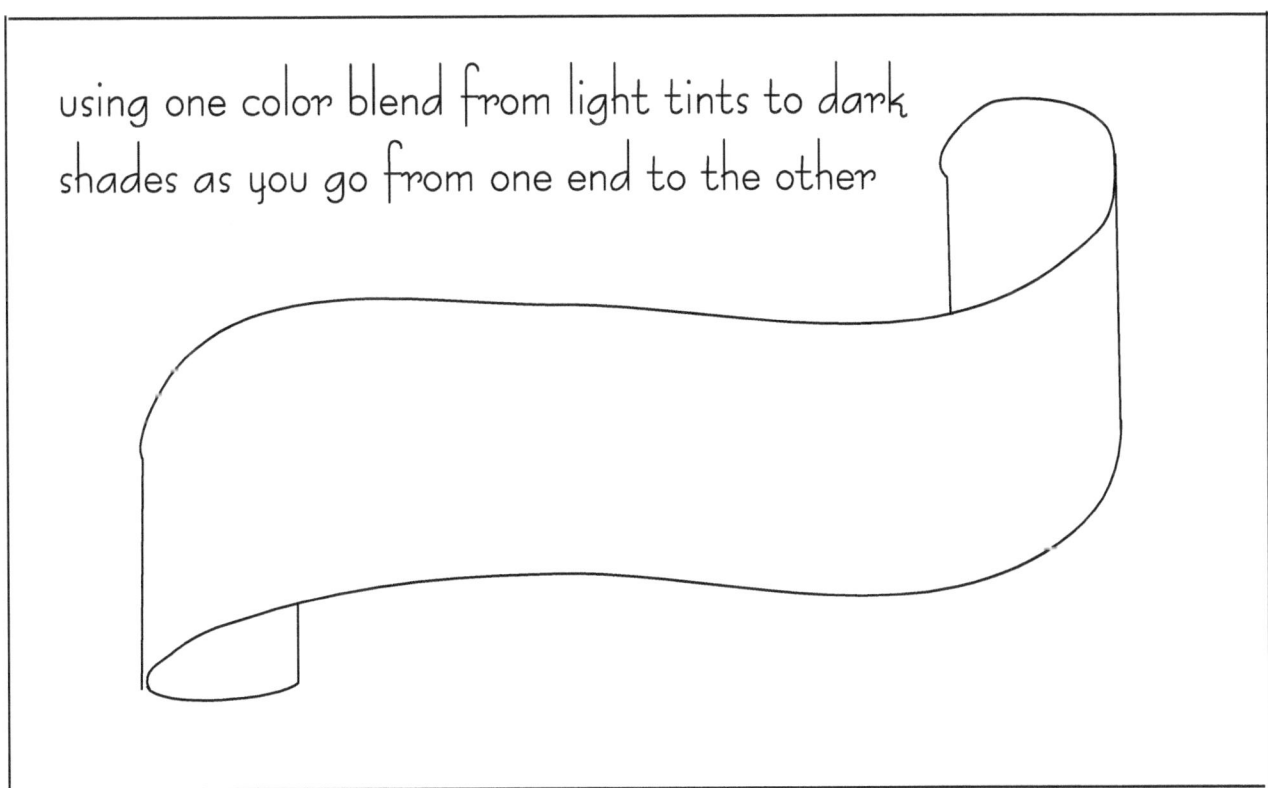

using one color blend from light tints to dark
shades as you go from one end to the other

color using value shading with color pencils

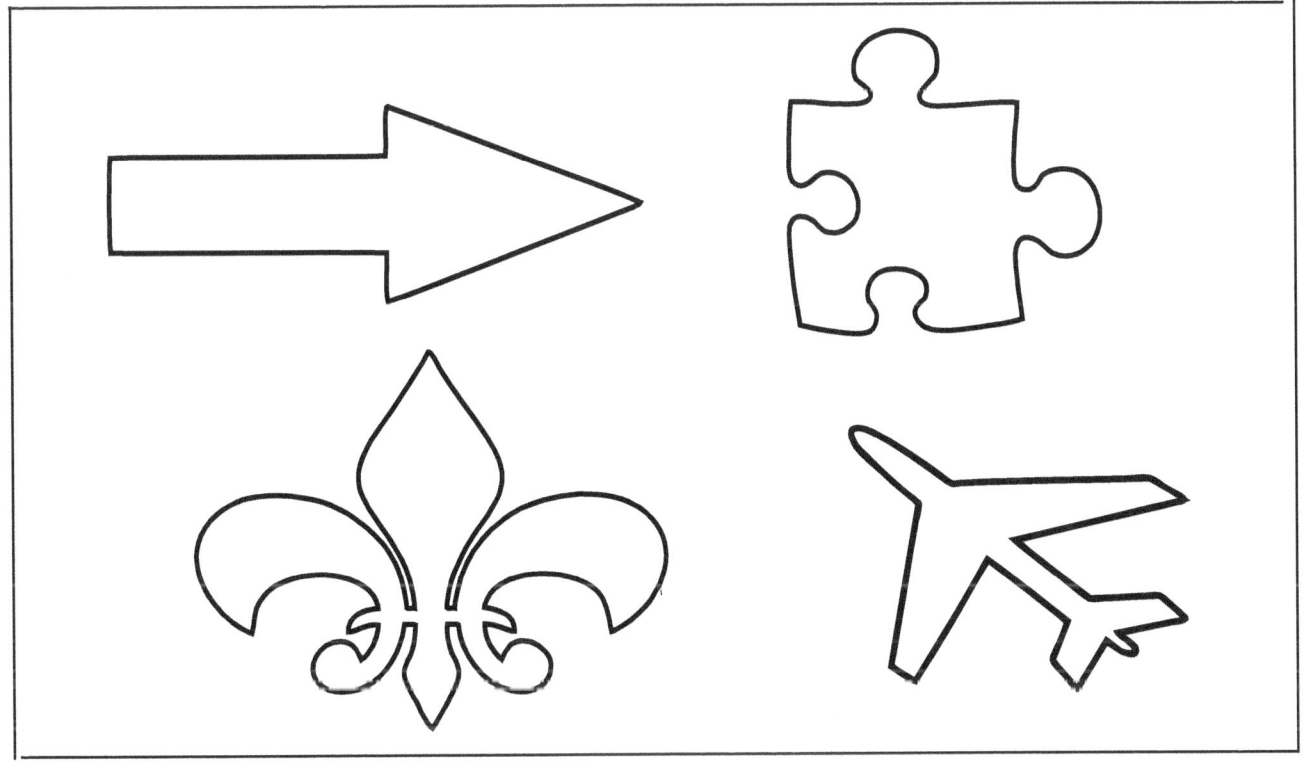

color using valuc shading with drawing pencil

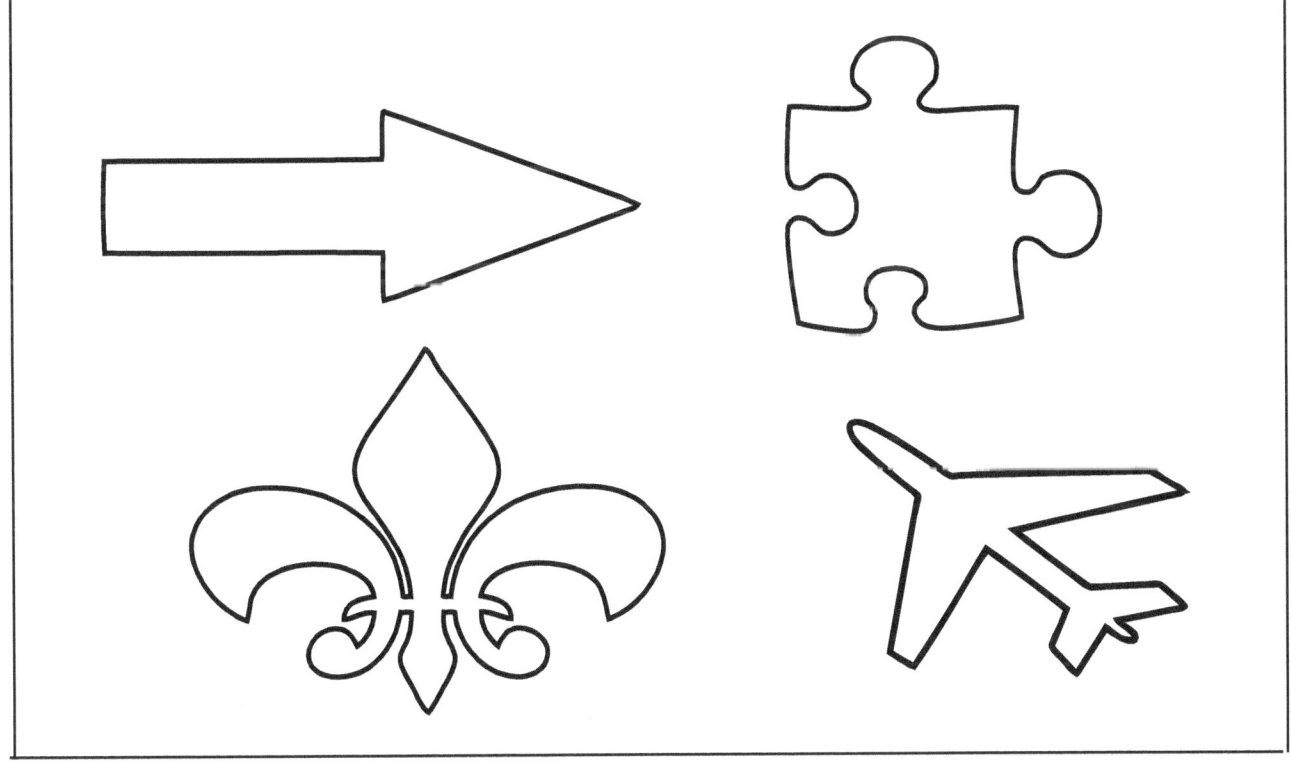

using a monochromatic color scheme
color this snail using tints and shades of blue/show blending

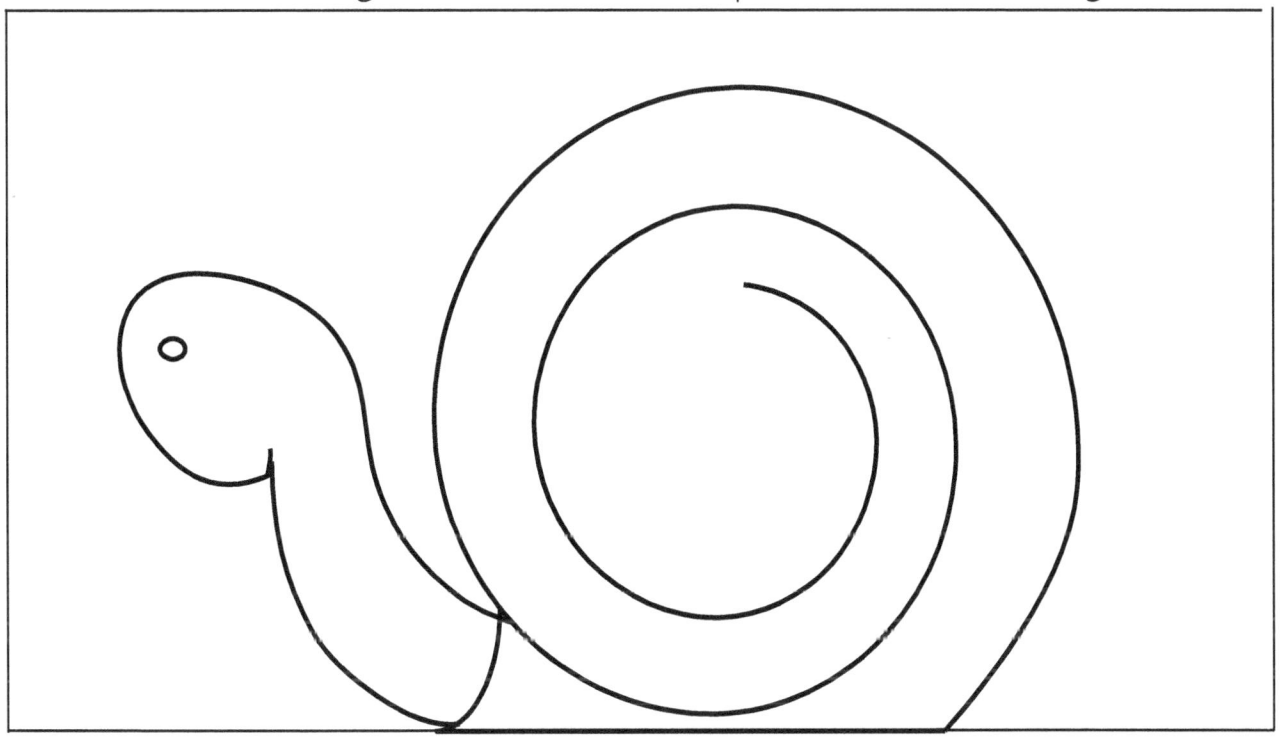

color this design with a color scheme & identify

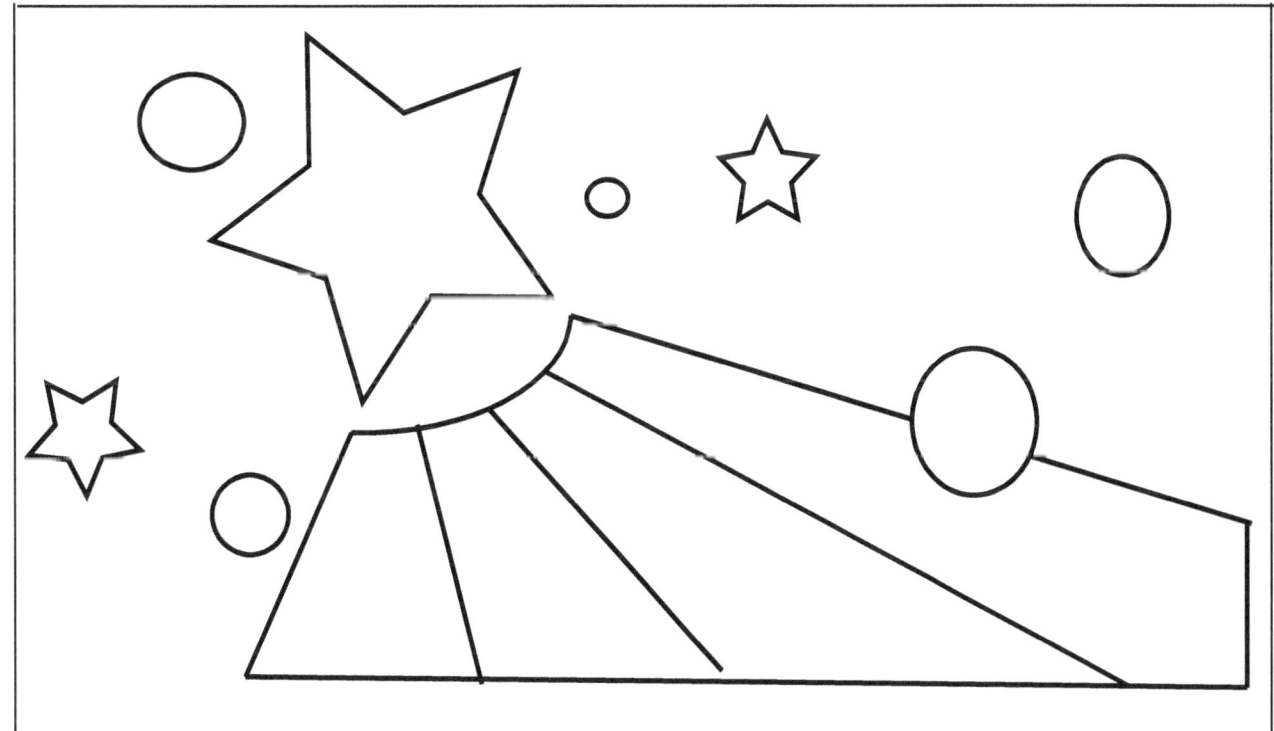

element of design - form
if you see the shape draw the form/ if you see the form draw the shape

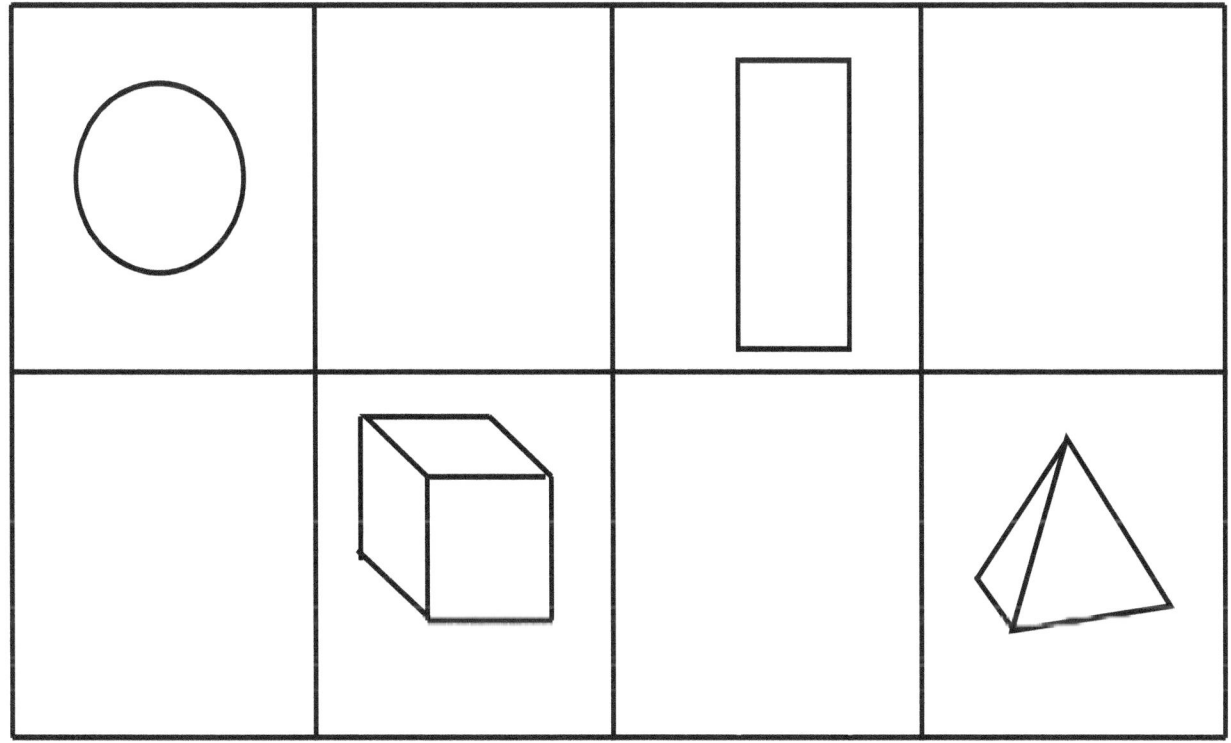

shape vs form
if you see the shape draw the form/ if you see the form draw the shape

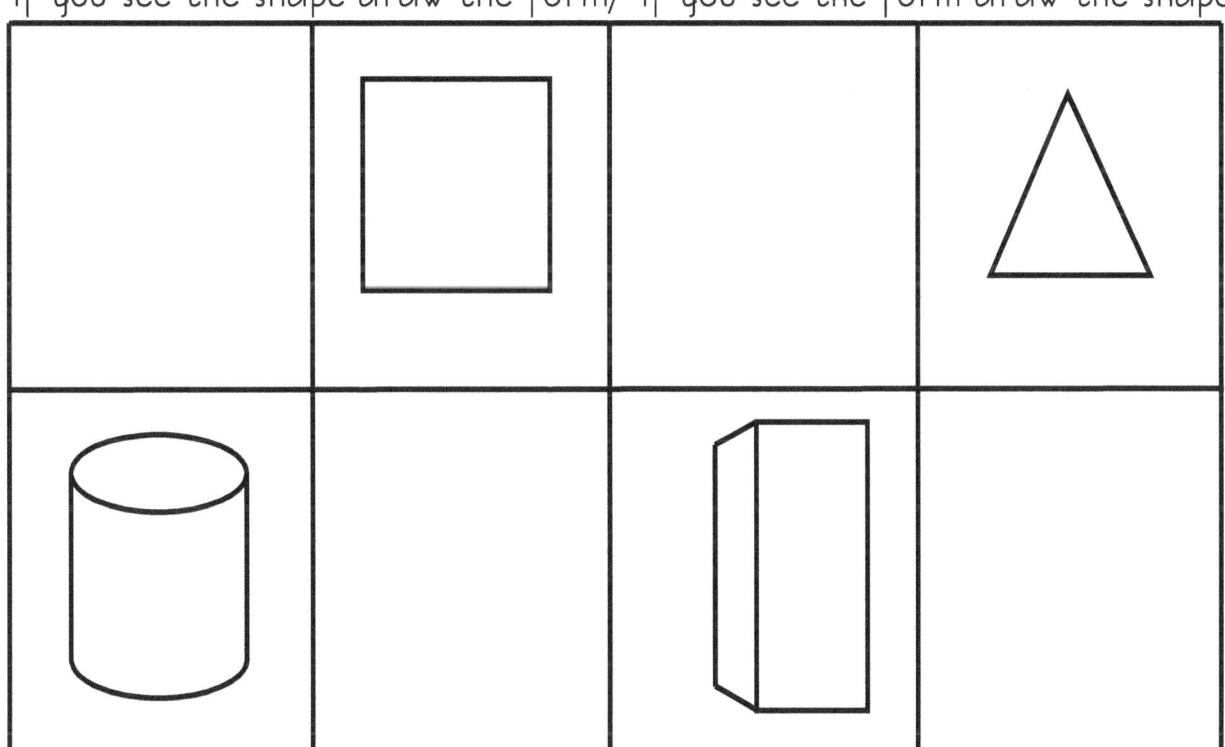

pencil shading - light source from the right

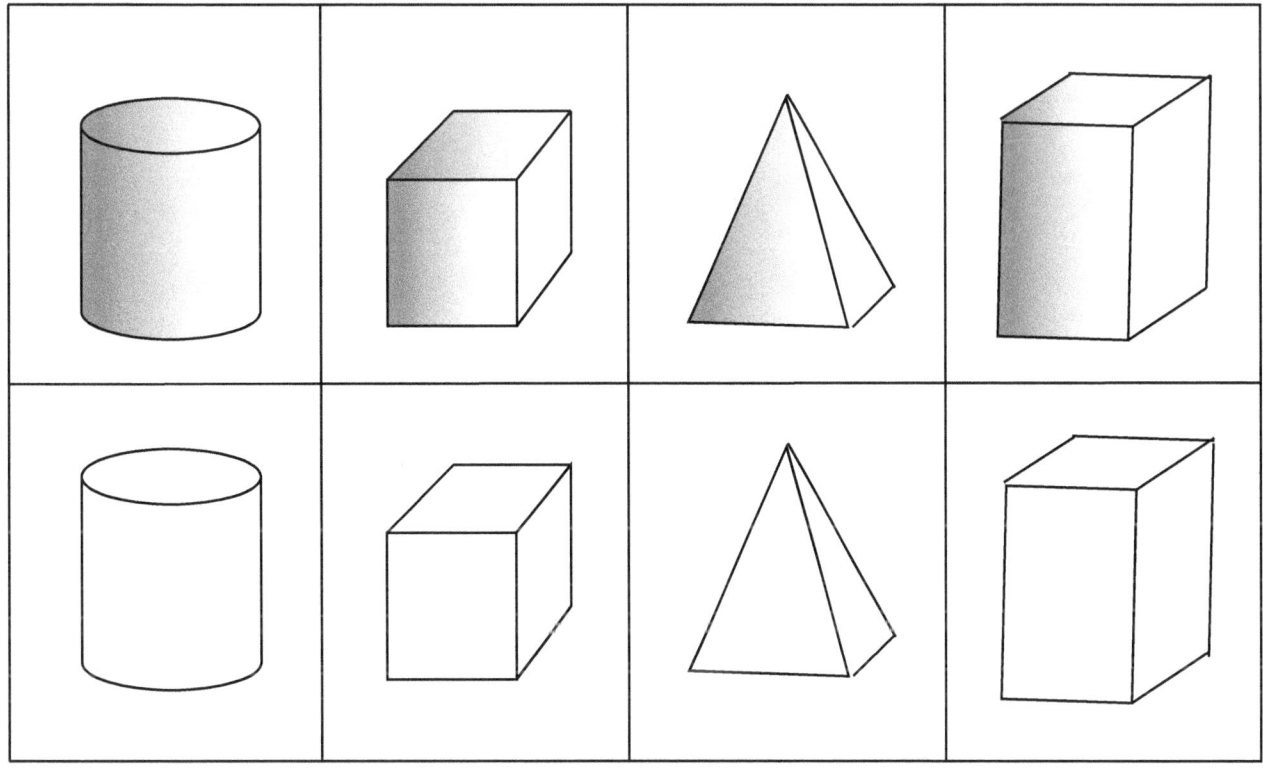

pencil shading

light source front	light source right	light source left	light source top

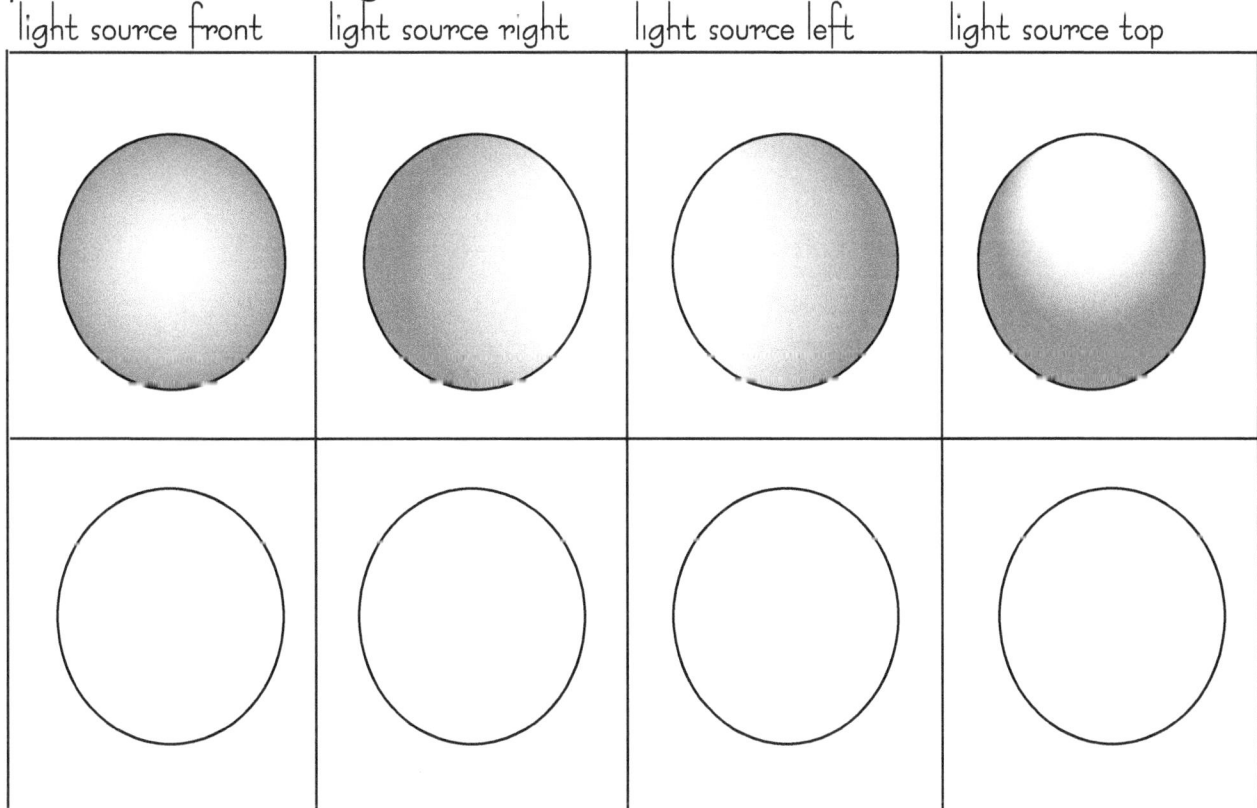

ink shading - light source from the right

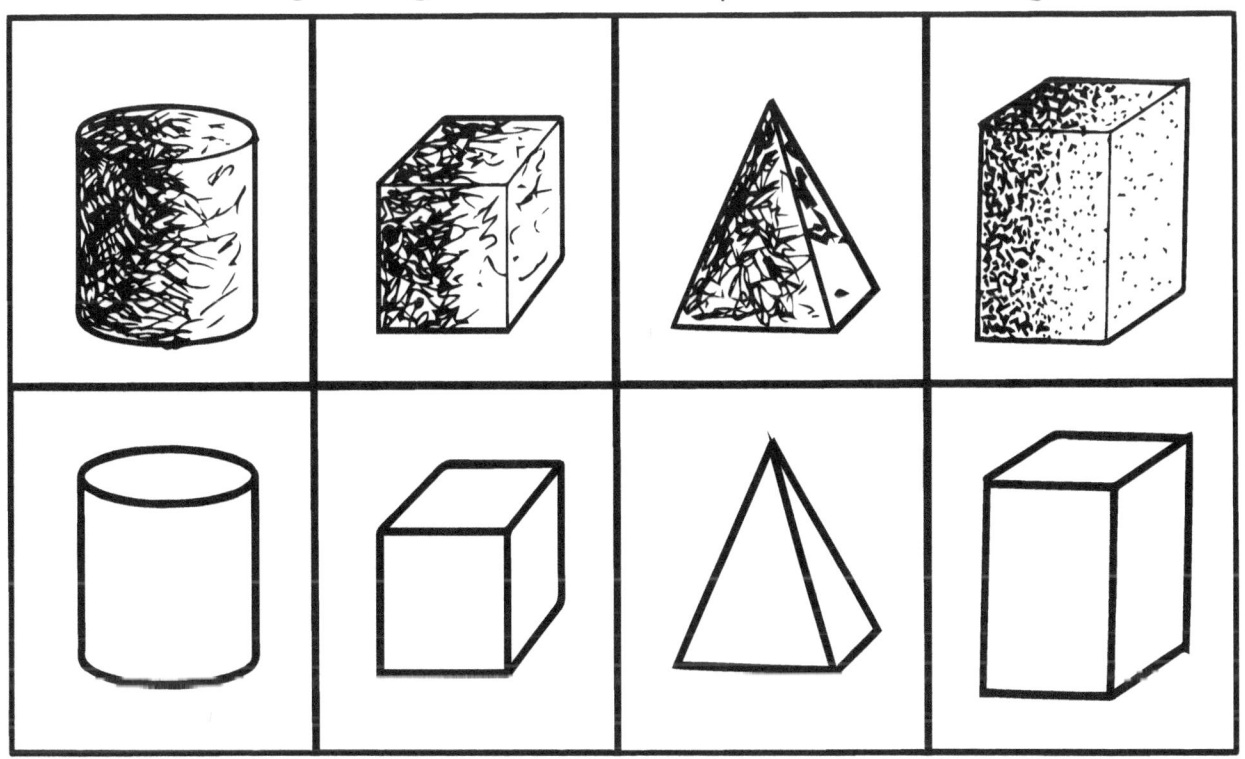

ink shading

light source front	light source right	light source left	light source top
squiggles	dots	lines	crosshatching

art
starts

principles of design

principle of design - balance
draw a design that shows symmetrical and asymmetrical balance

symmetrical

asymmetrical

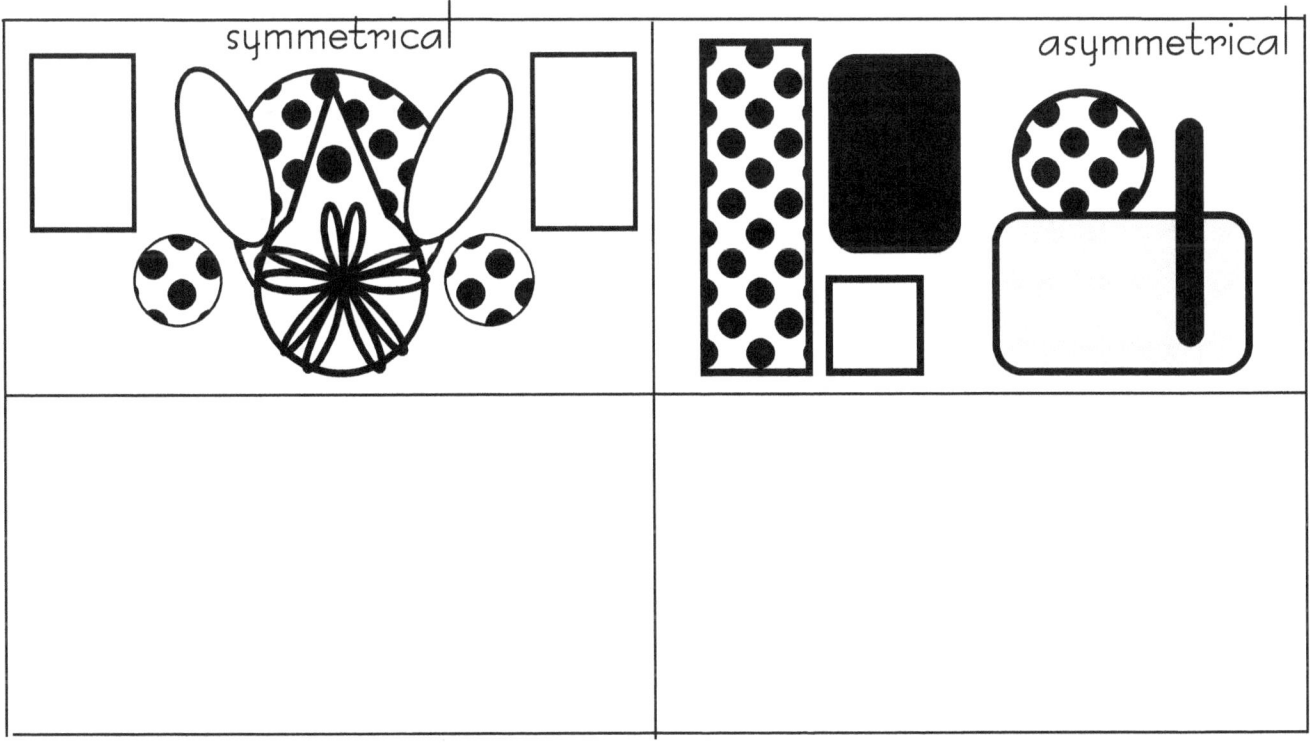

principle of design - harmony
draw three designs that show harmony

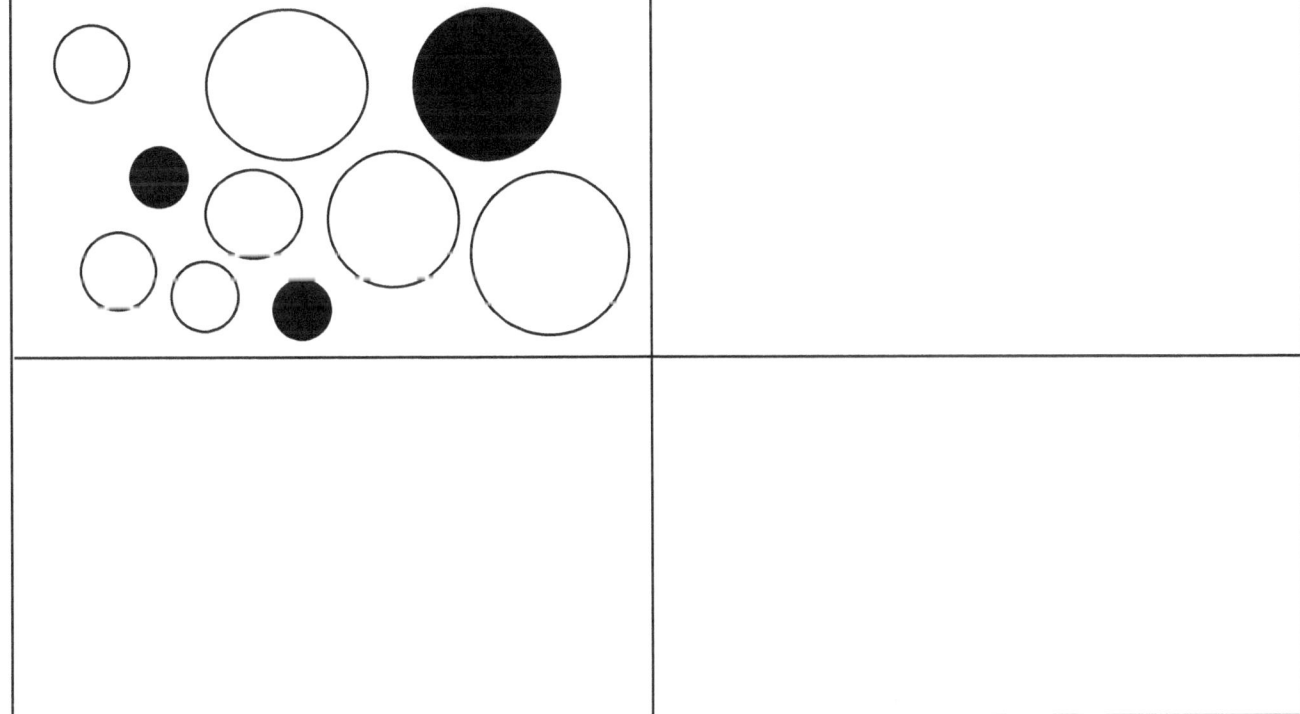

principle of design - repetition
draw three designs that show repetition

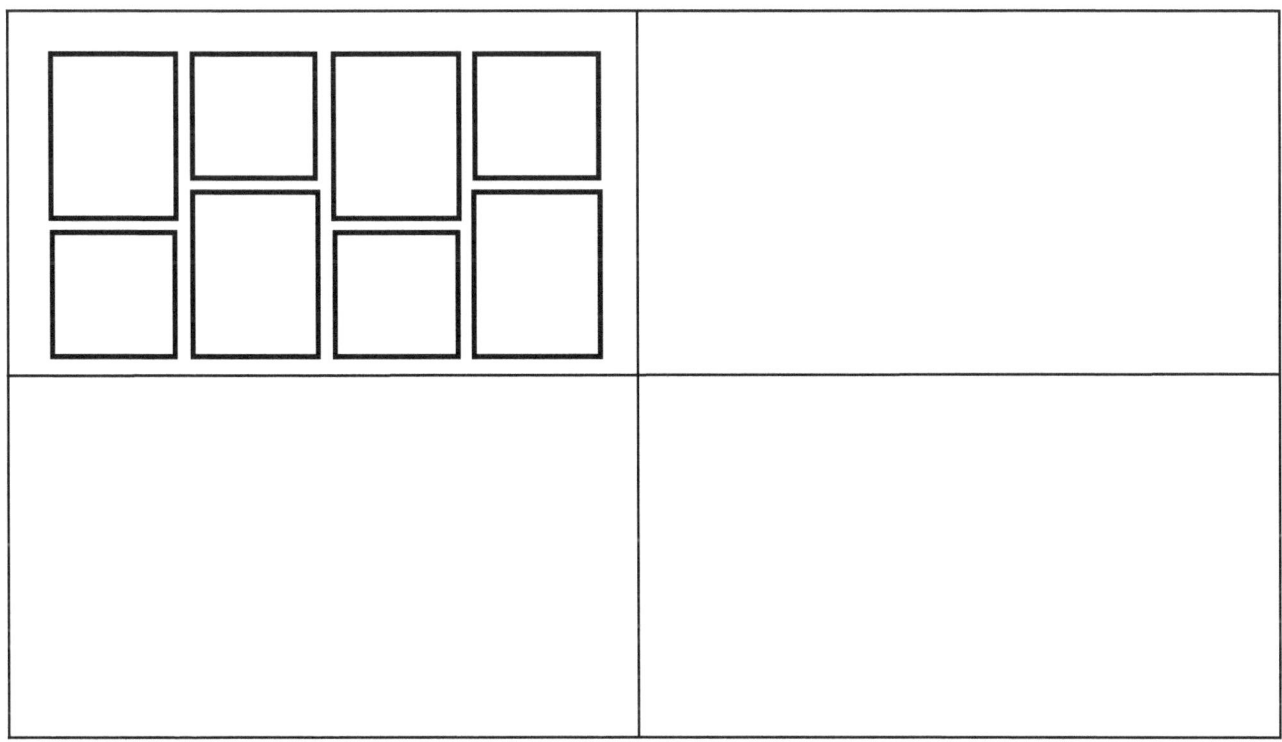

principle of design - emphasis
draw two designs that show emphasis

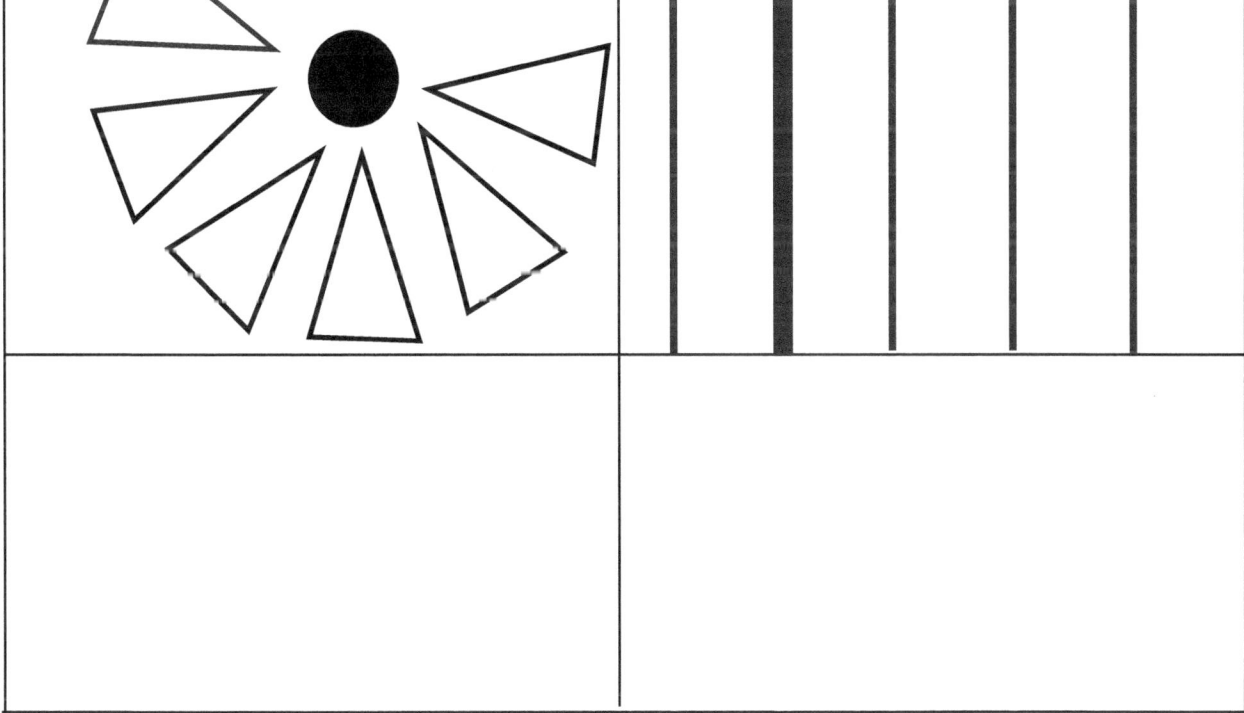

principle of design - contrast
draw two designs that show contrast

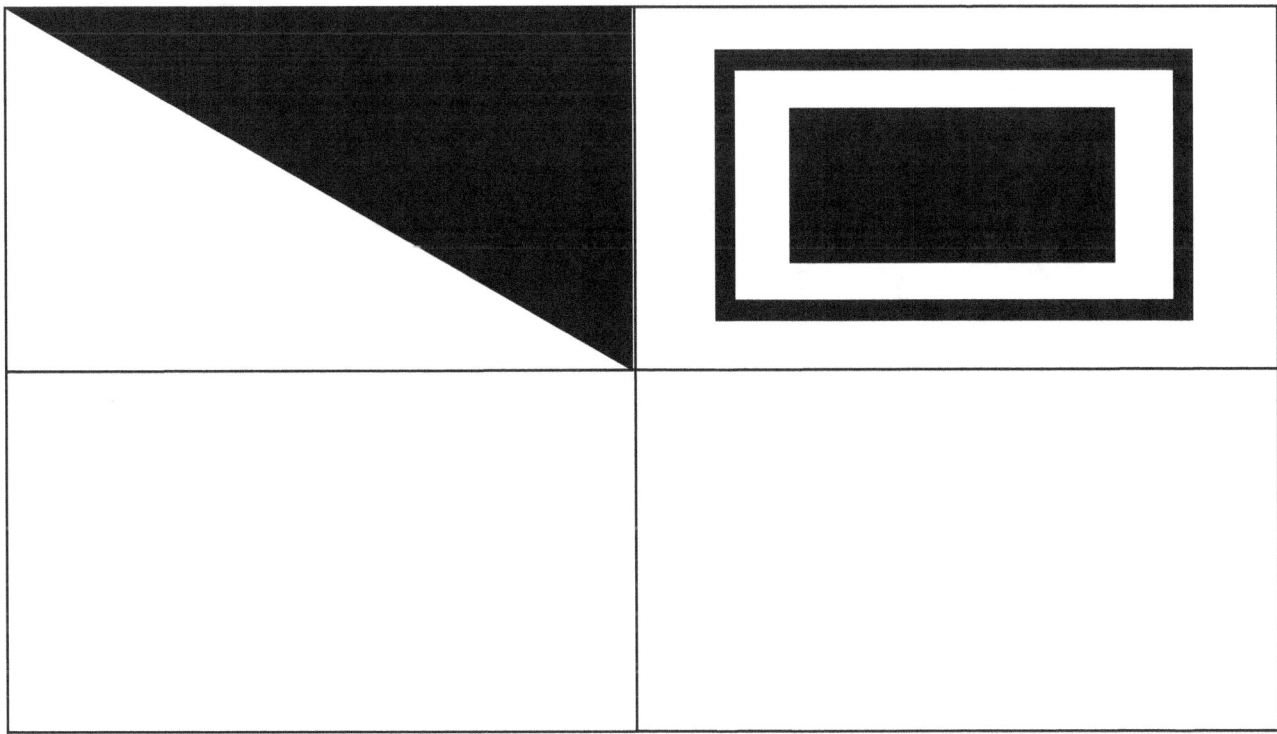

principle of design - rhythm
draw three designs that show rhythm

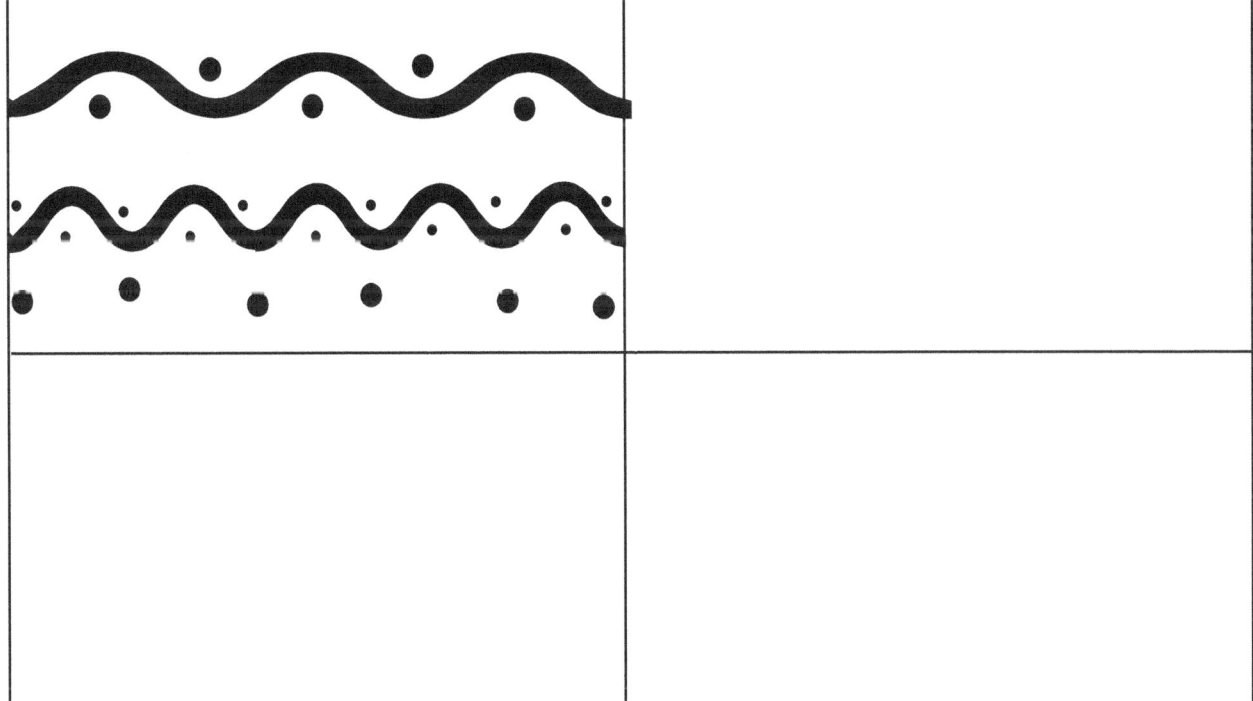

art
starts
drawing activities

it's all about the detail

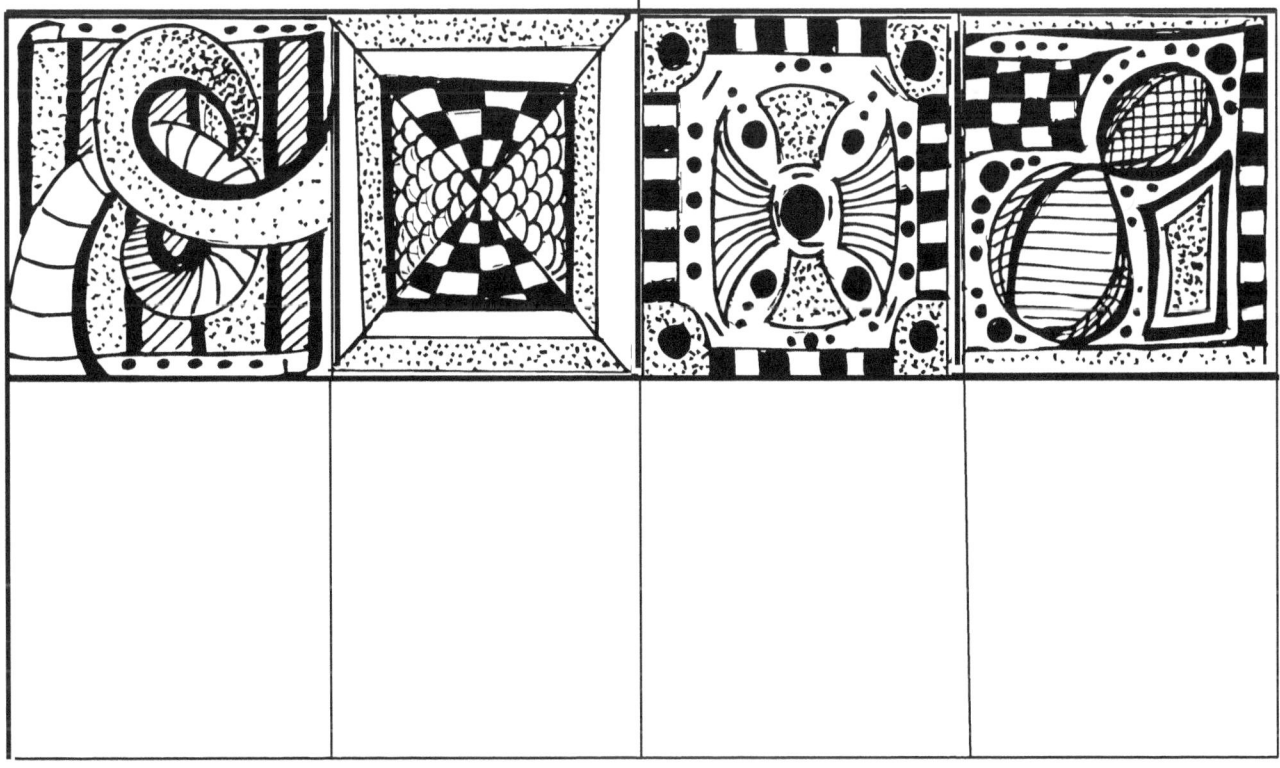

paisley patterns

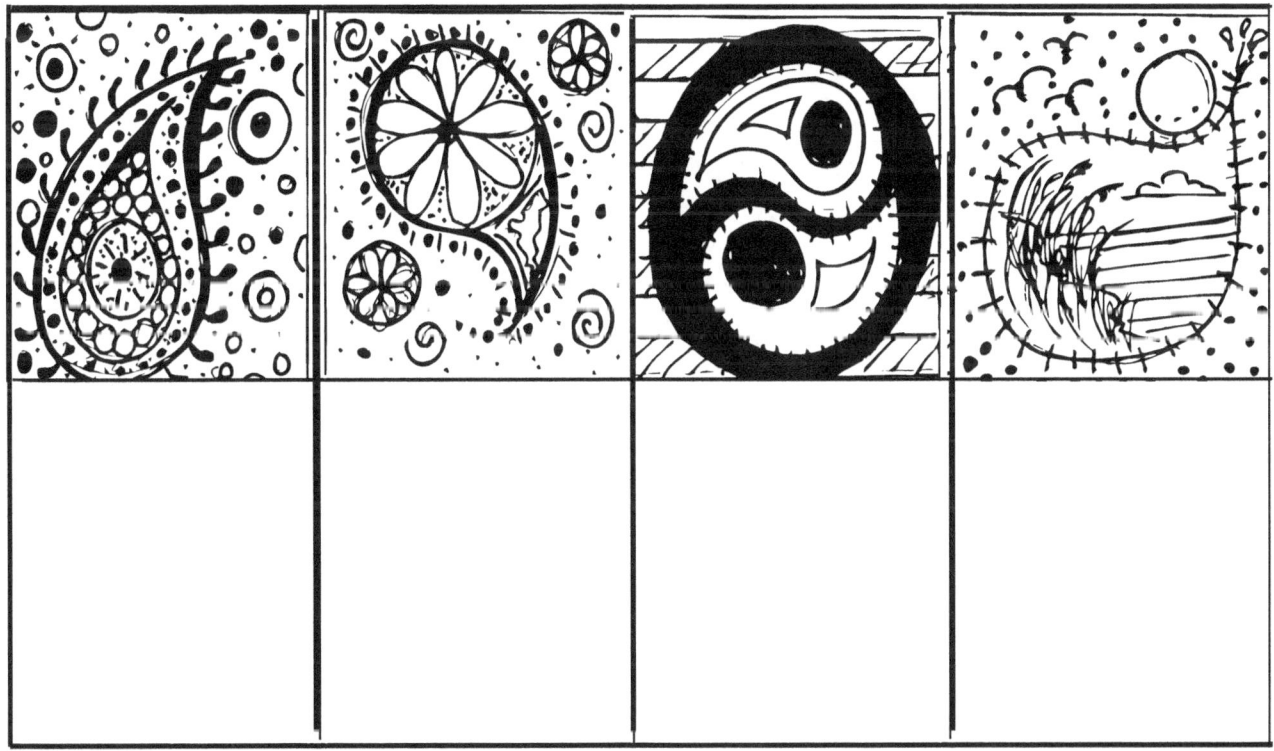

draw what you see

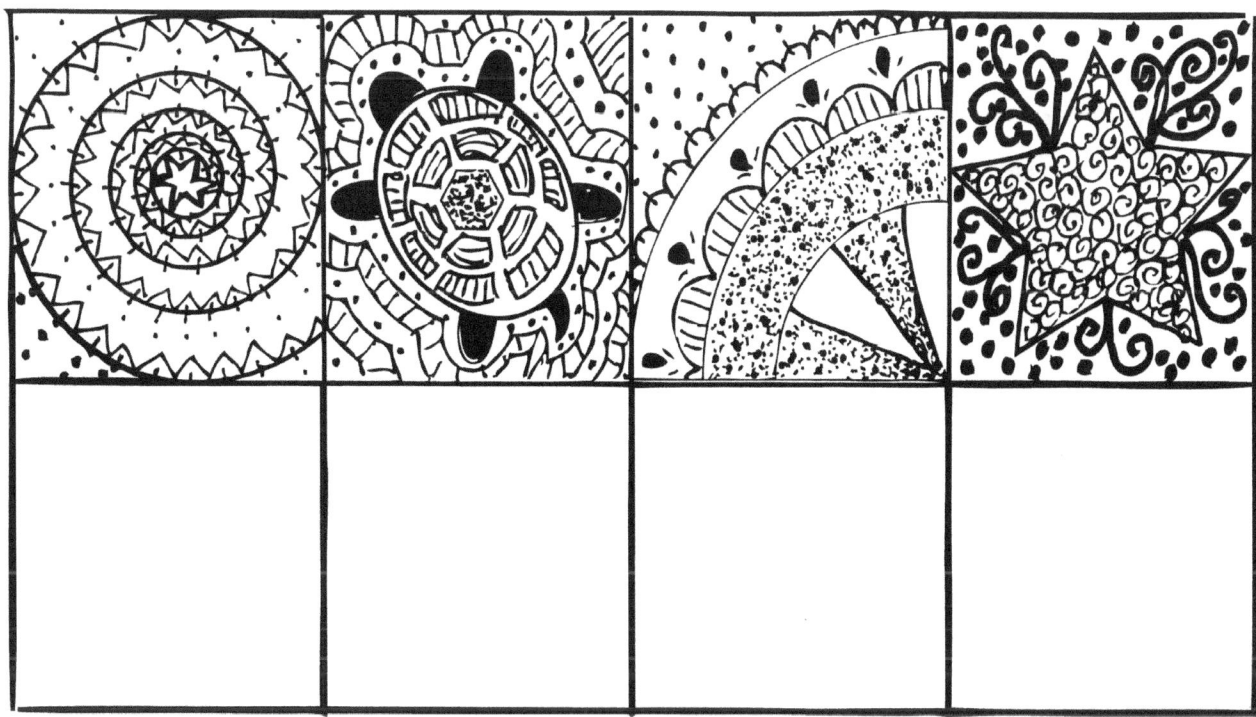

drawing the details

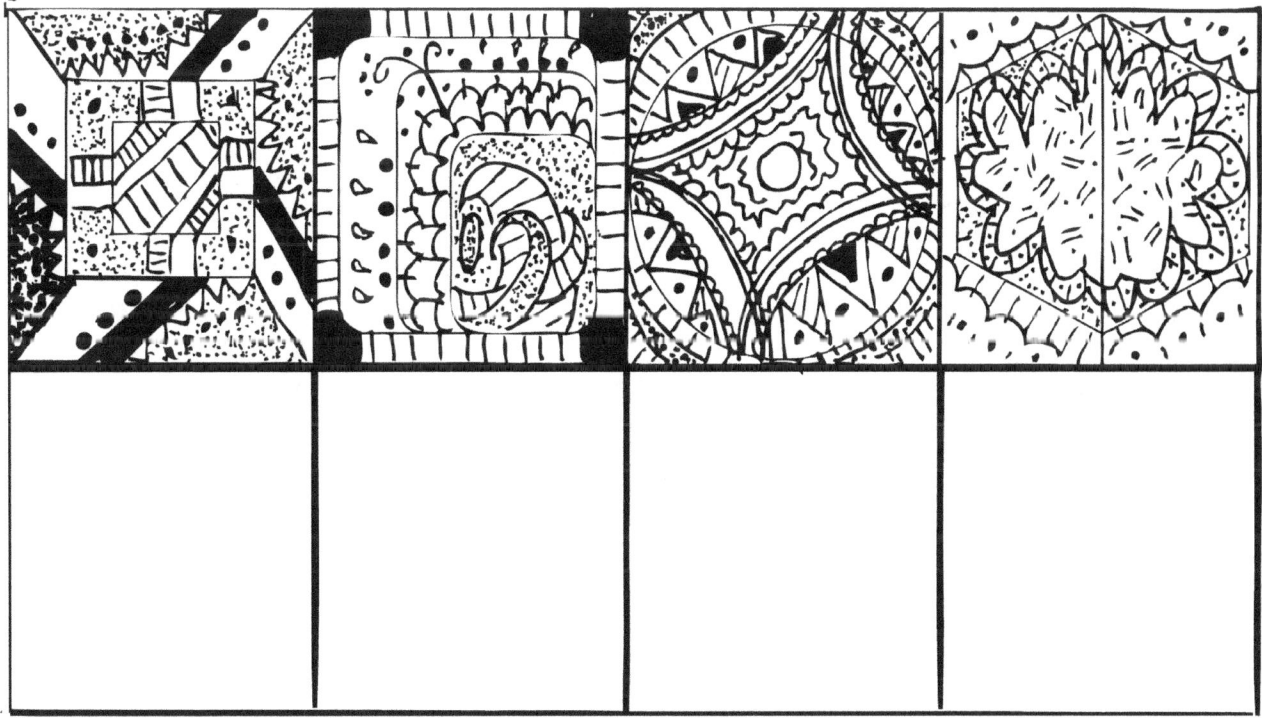

copy the drawing or draw something similar

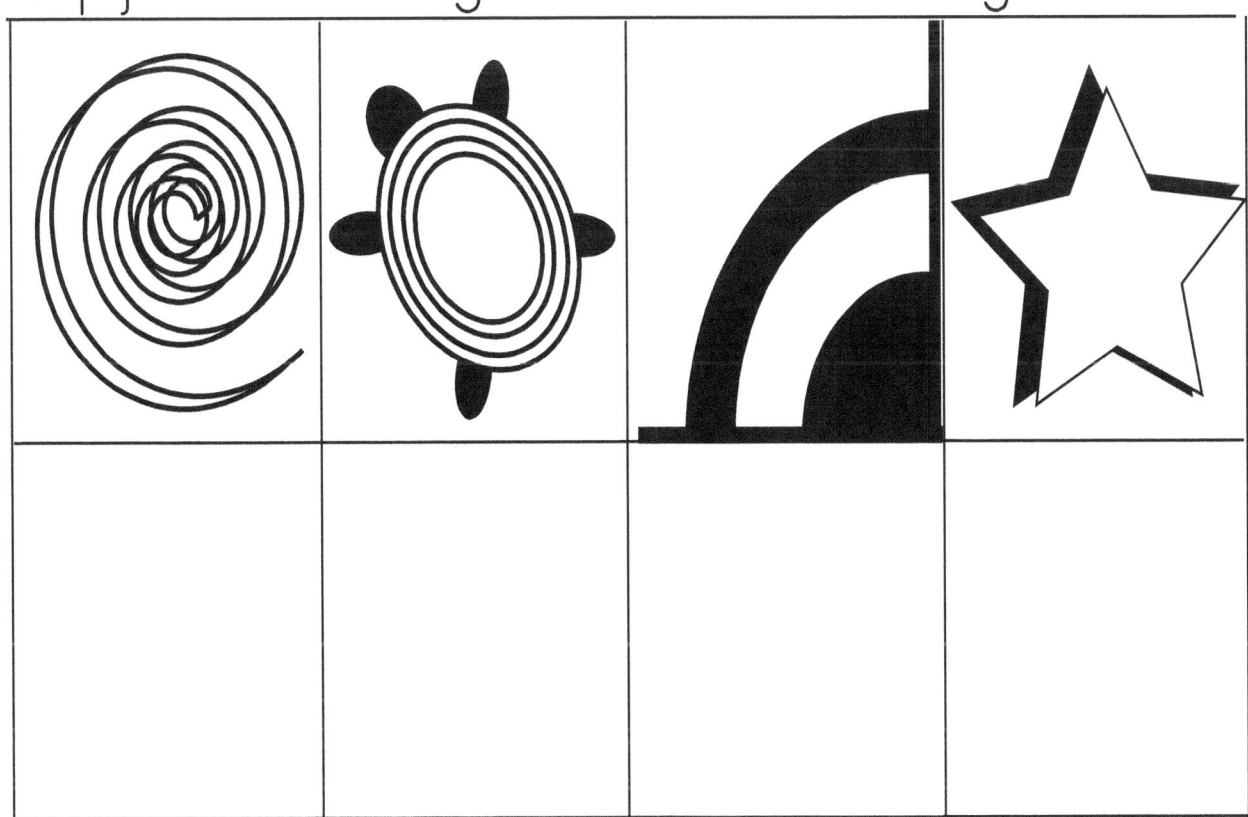

copy the drawing or draw something similar

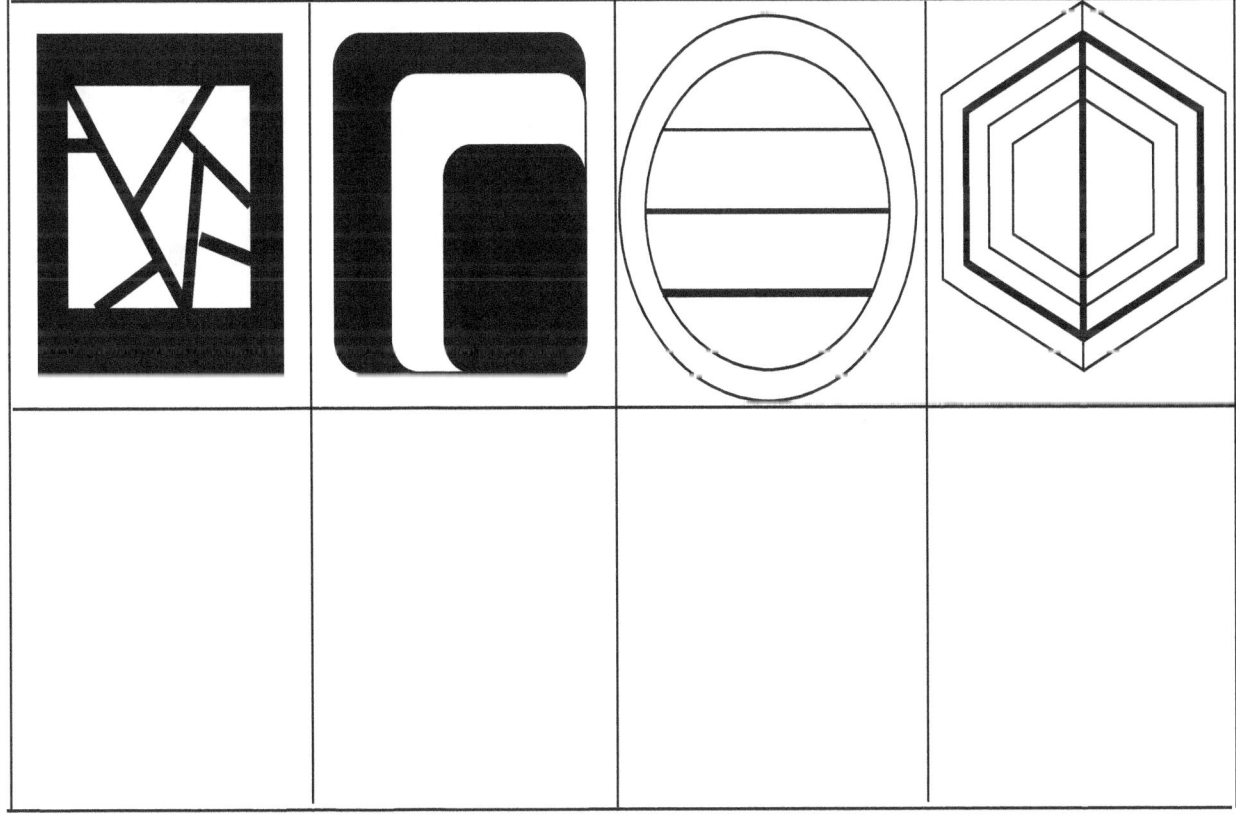

drawing angles and dots

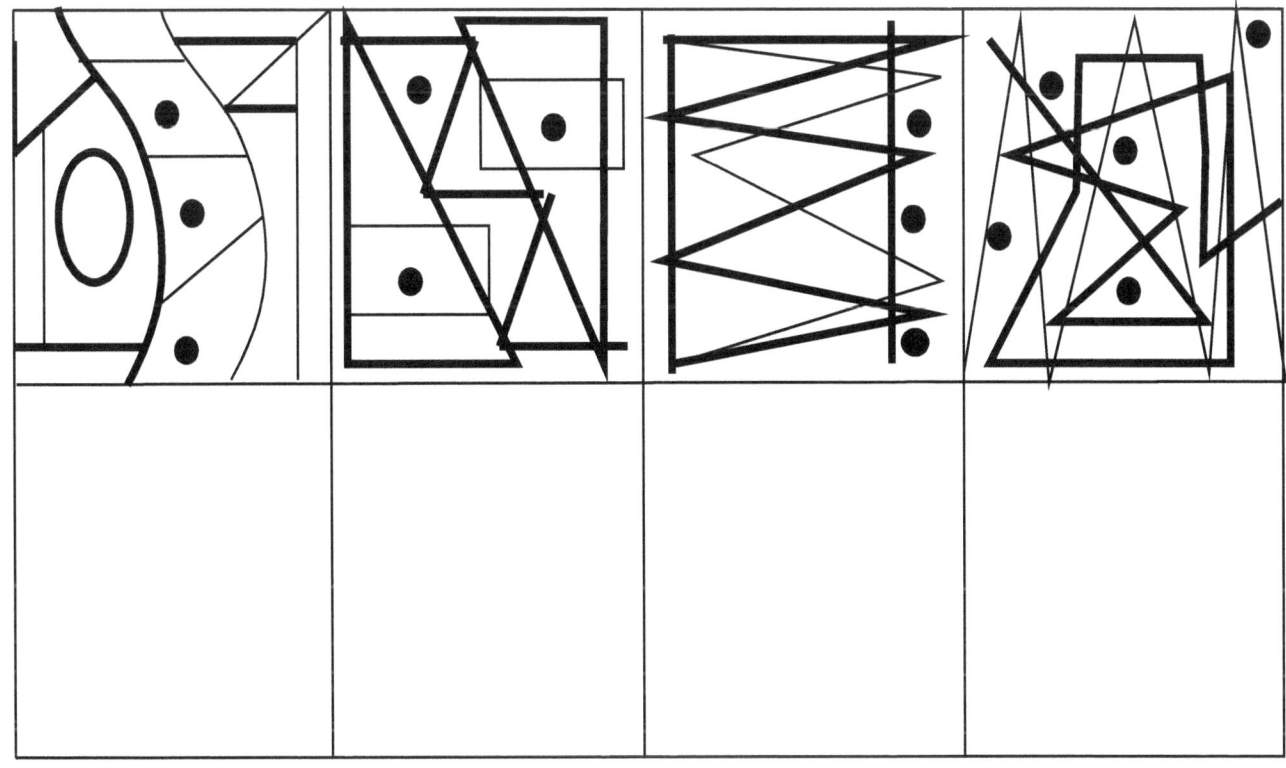

drawing curves and dots

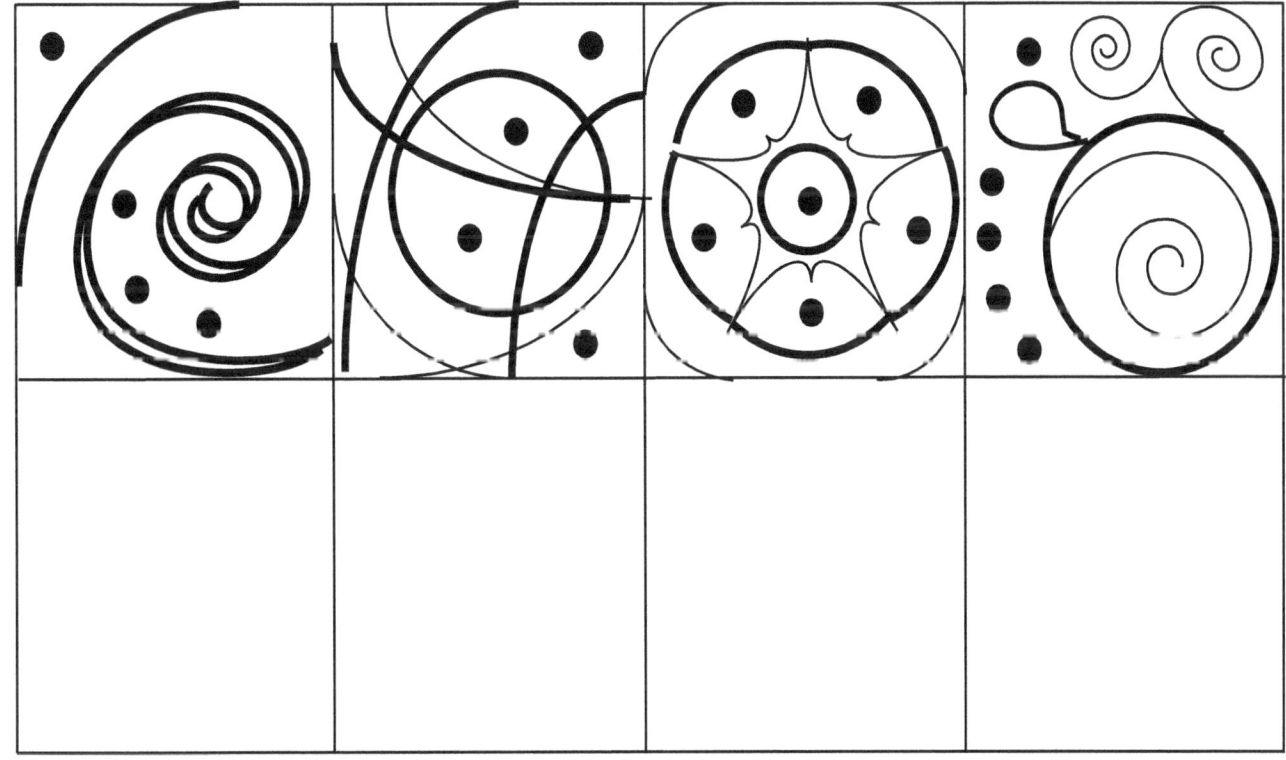

draw some flourishes

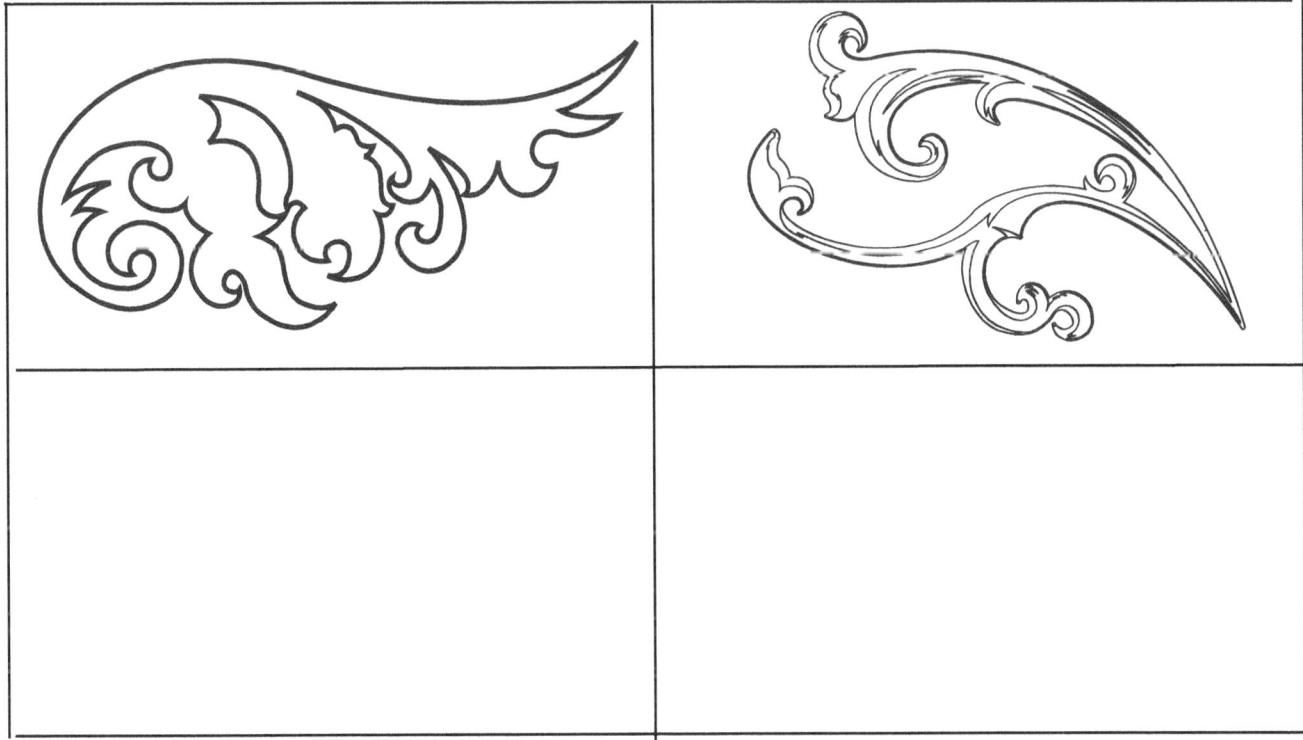

draw some swirls and dots

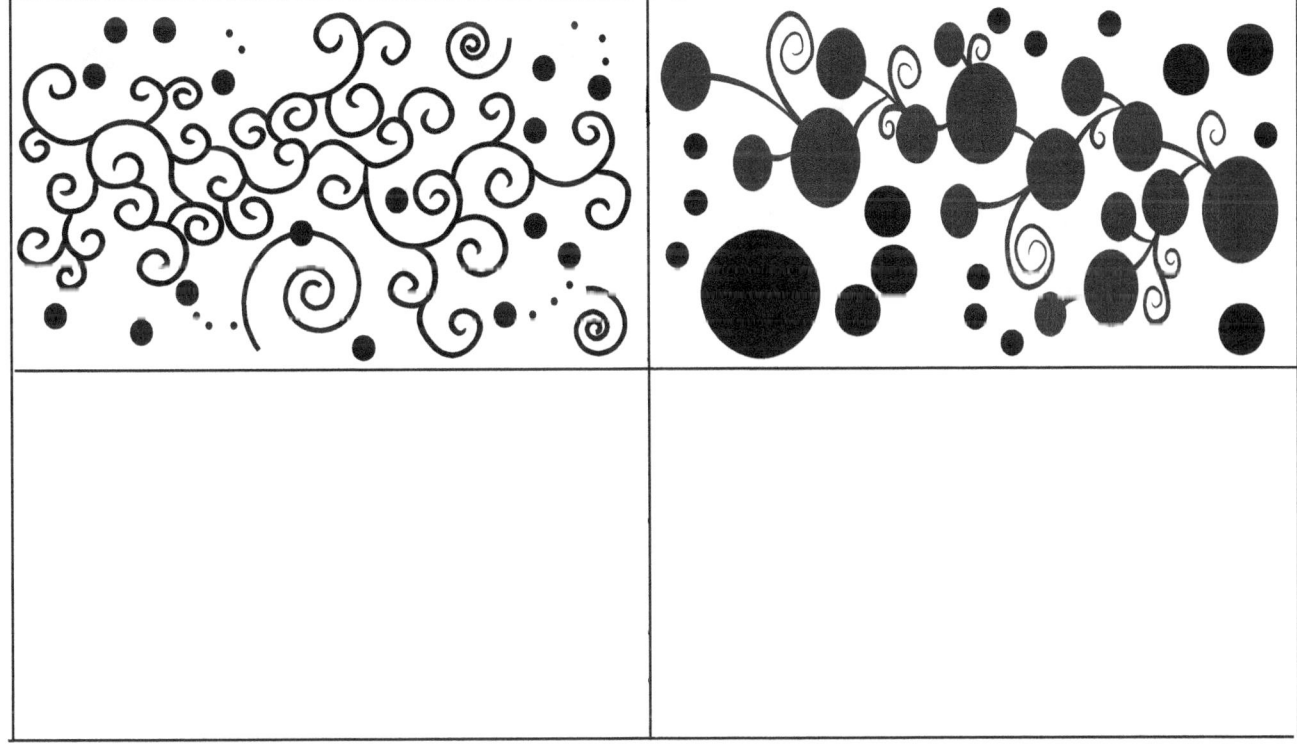

facial features

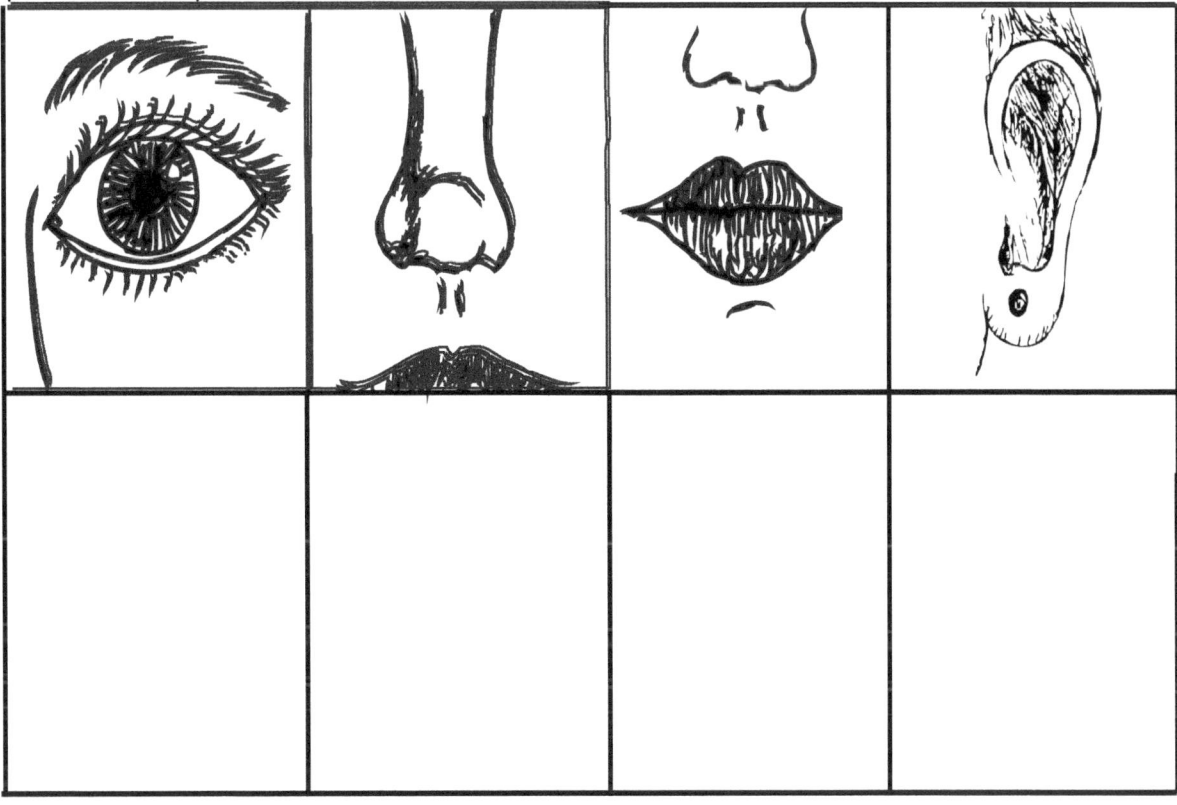

facial features

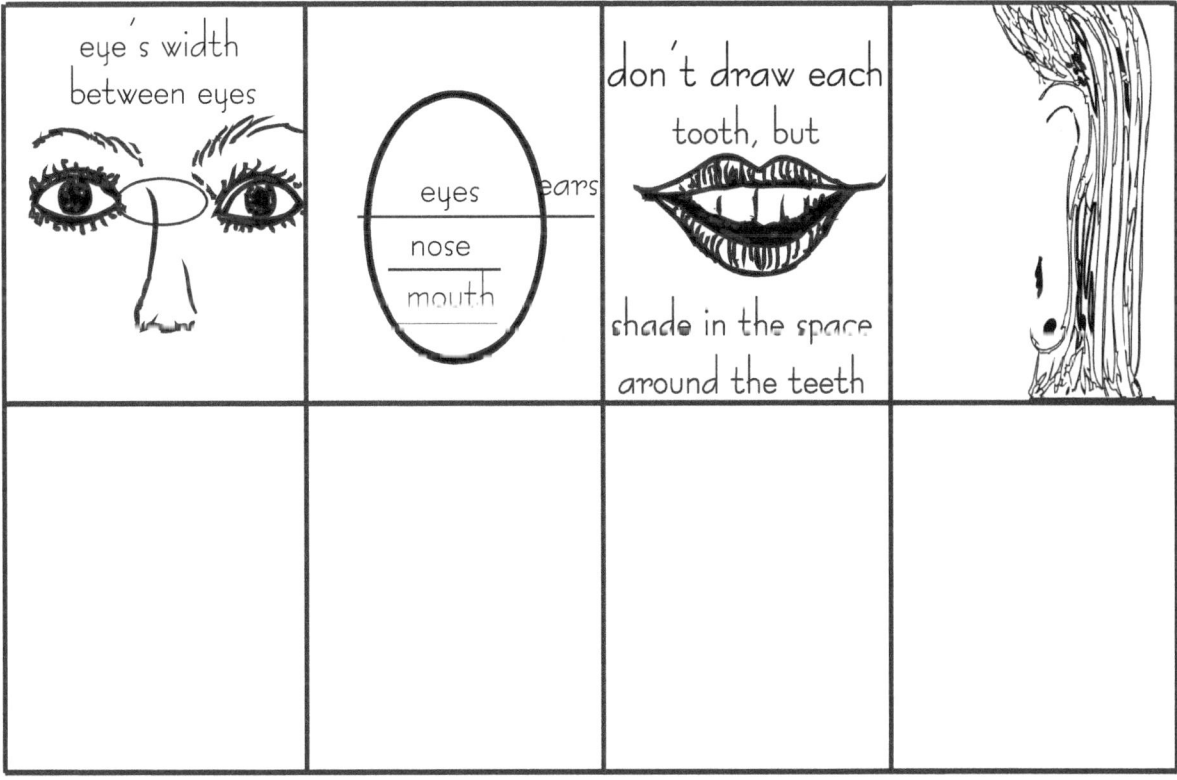

use all three of the lines to draw something, or use each
shape separately and draw three different objects

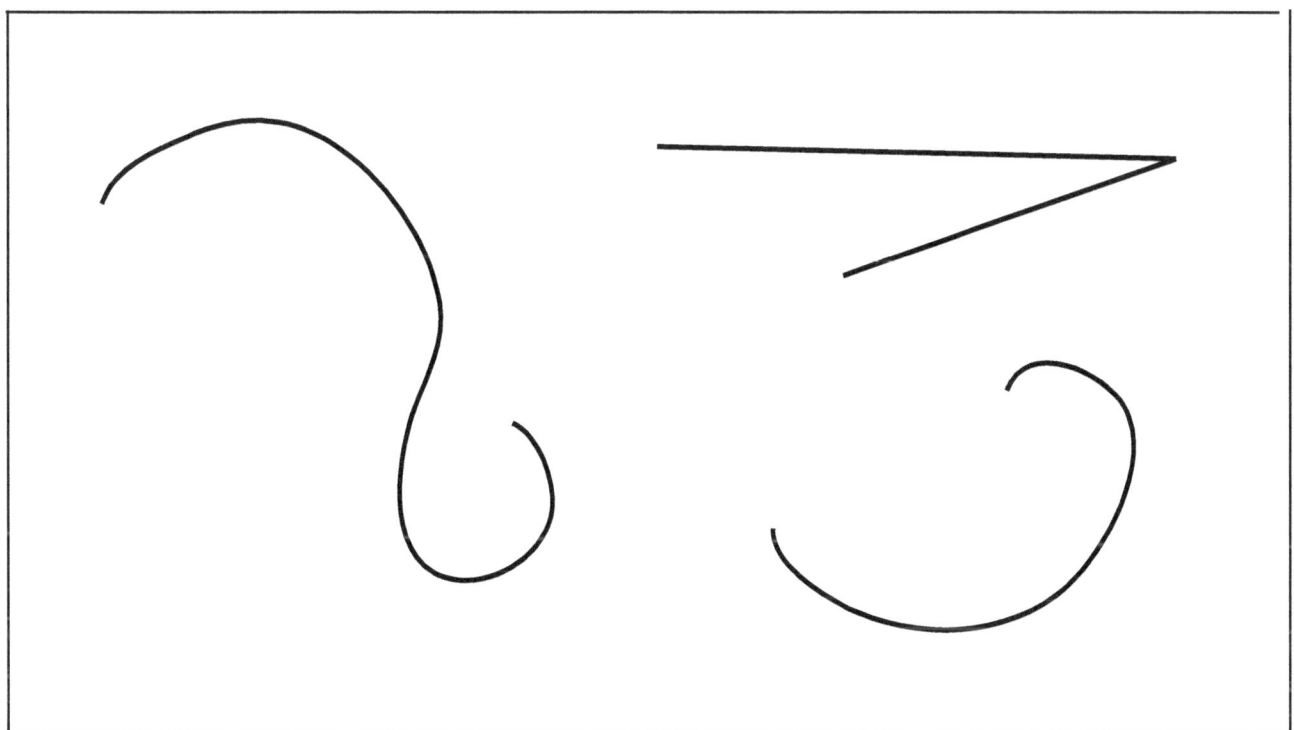

use all three of the shapes to draw something, or use each
shape separately and draw three different objects

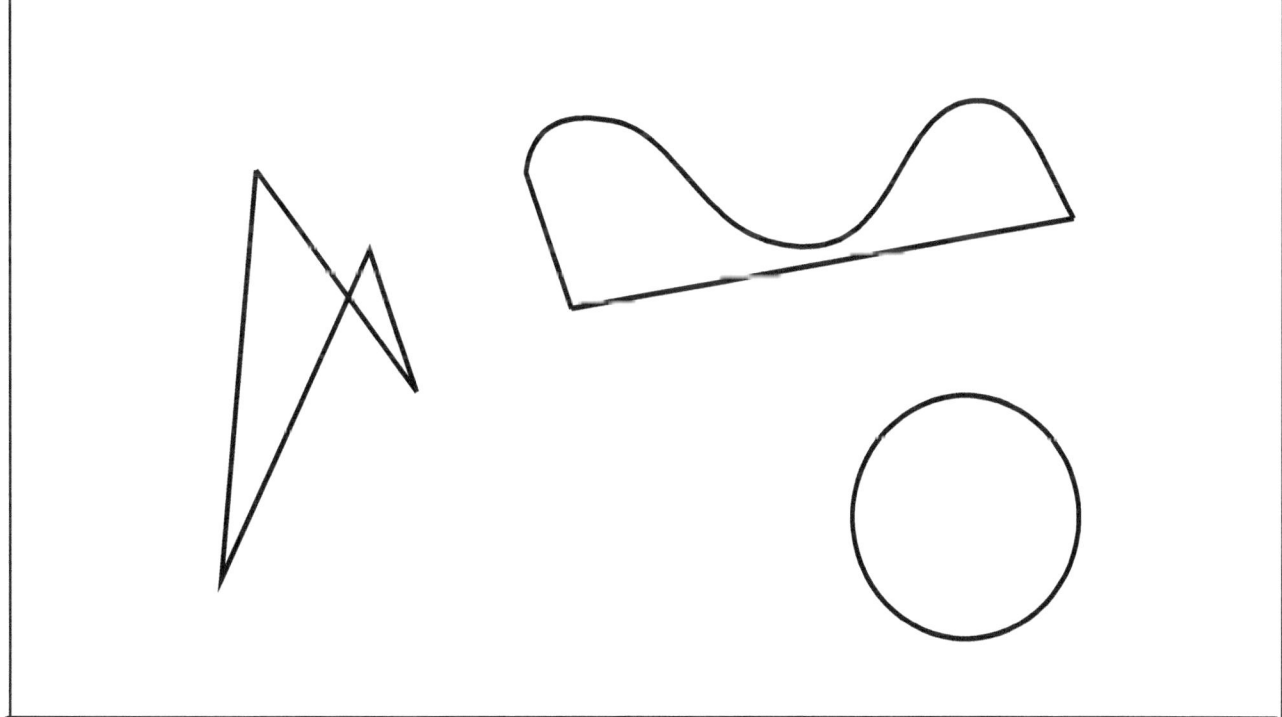

draw an animal using this squiggle

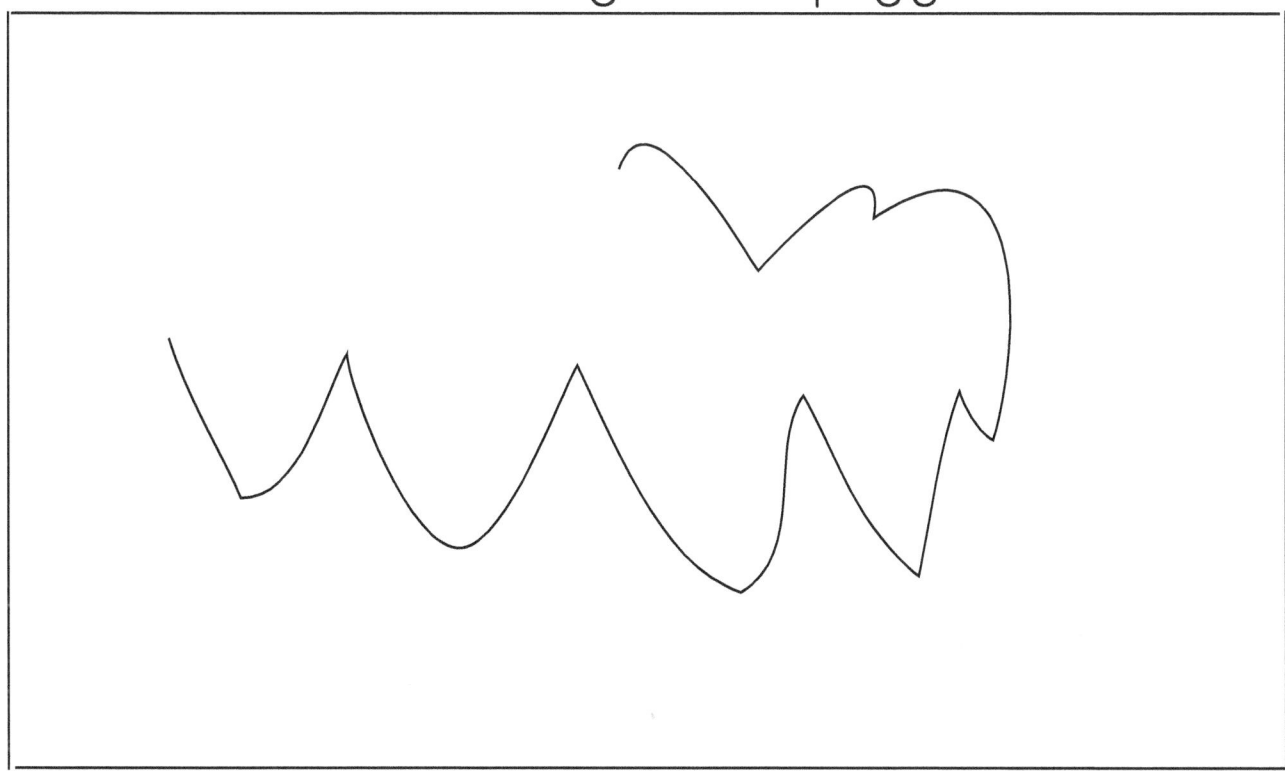

draw anything using this squiggle

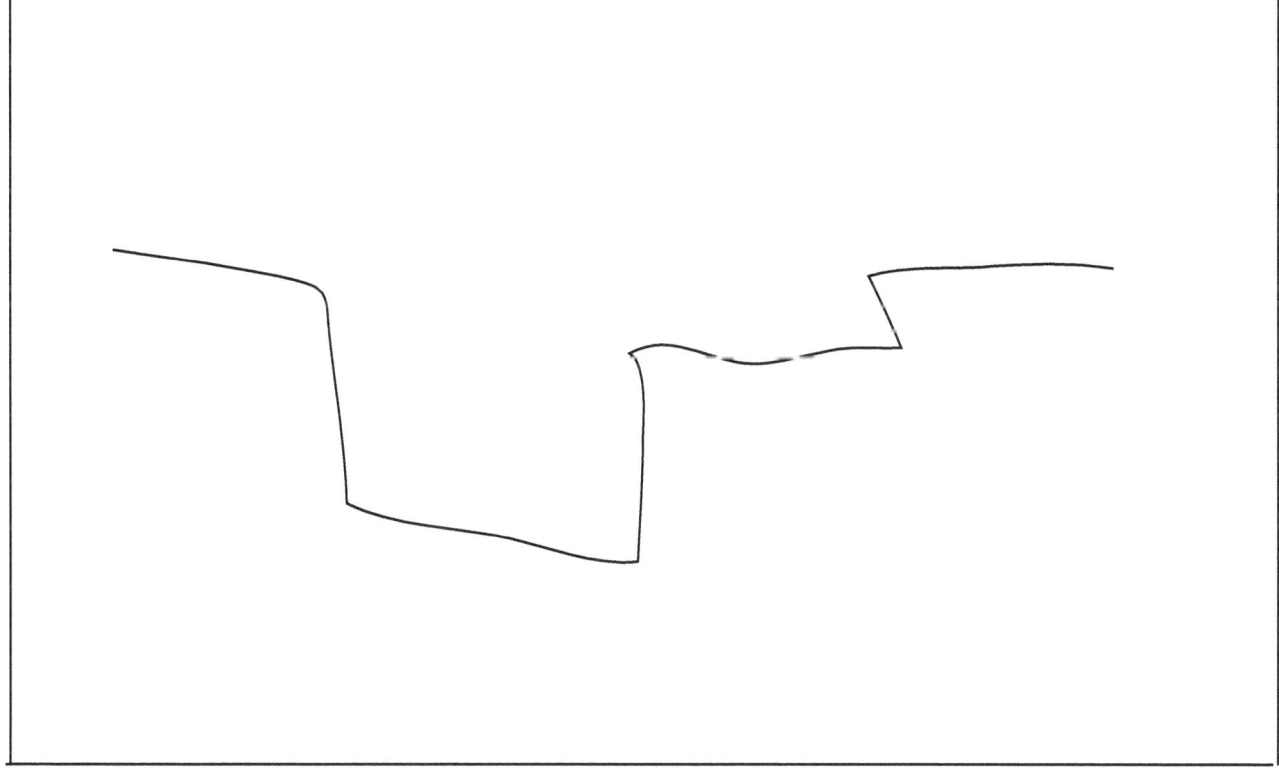

use all three of the lines to draw something, or use each
shape separately and draw three different objects

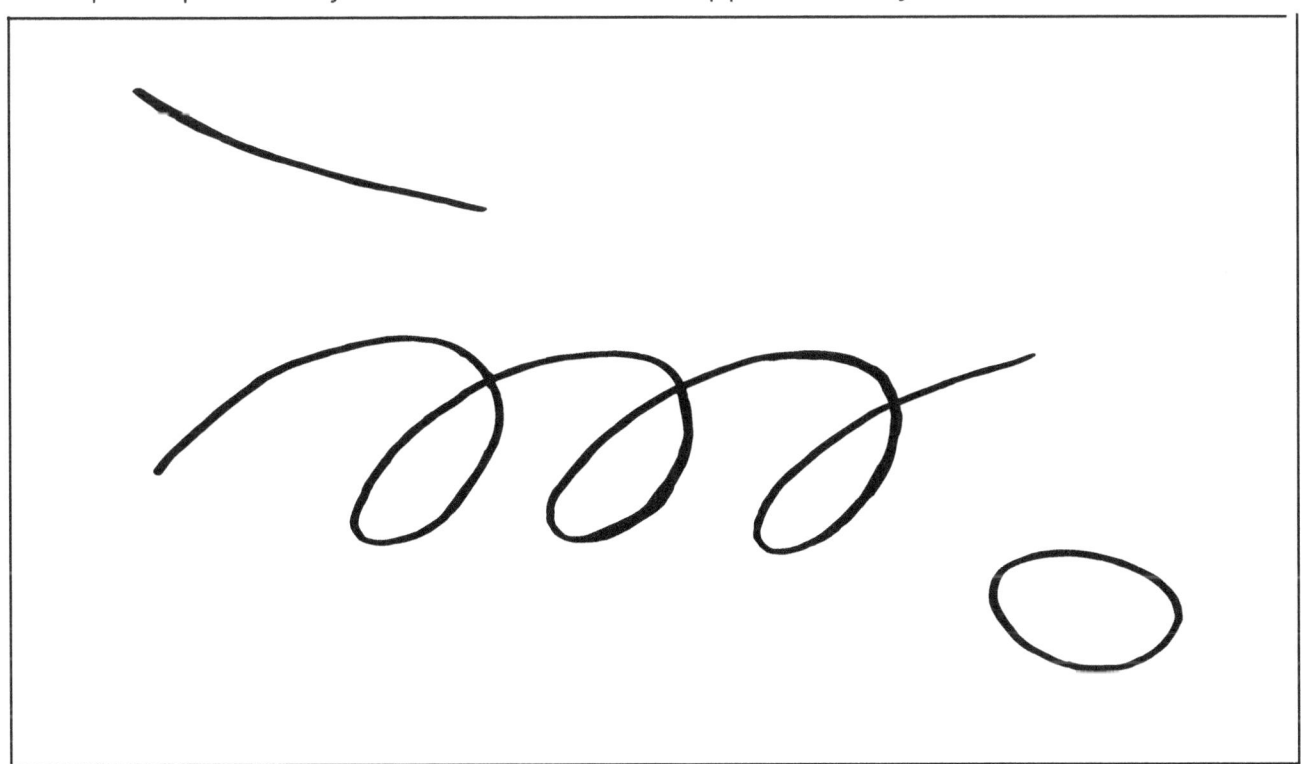

use all three of the shapes to draw something, or use each
shape separately and draw three different objects

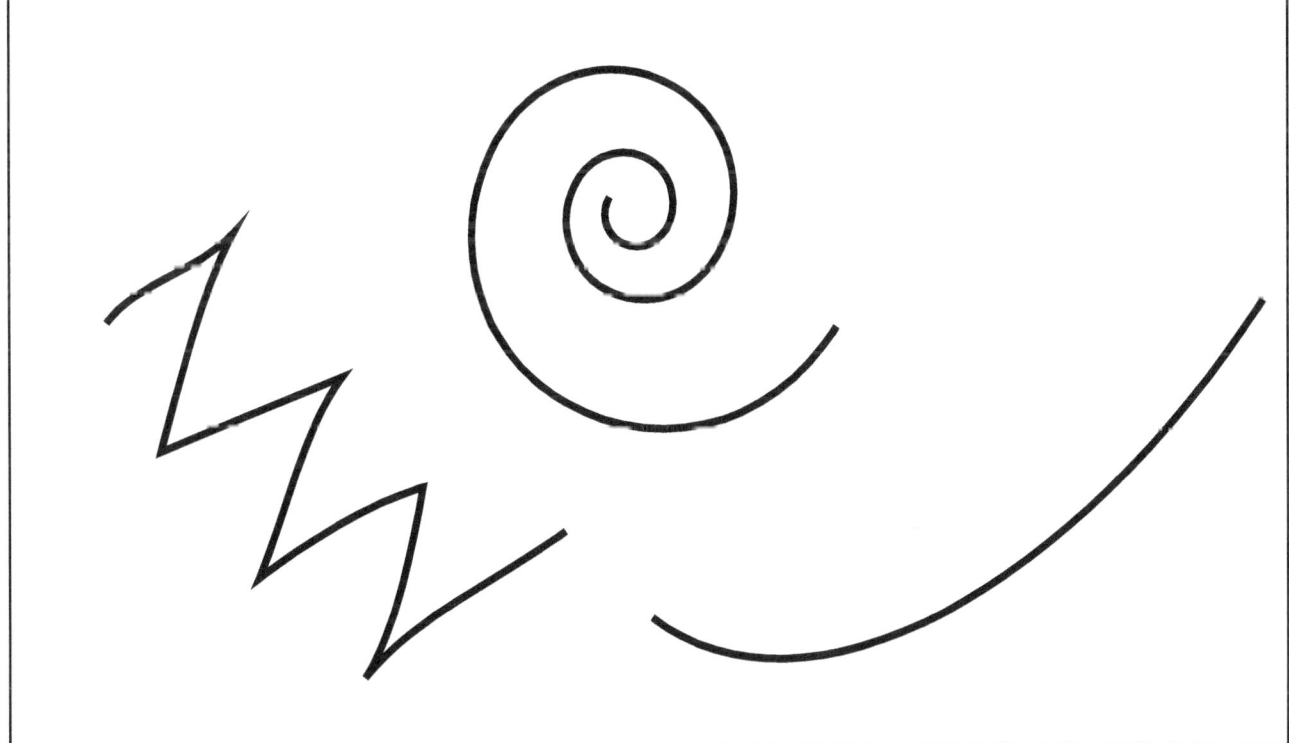

symbols

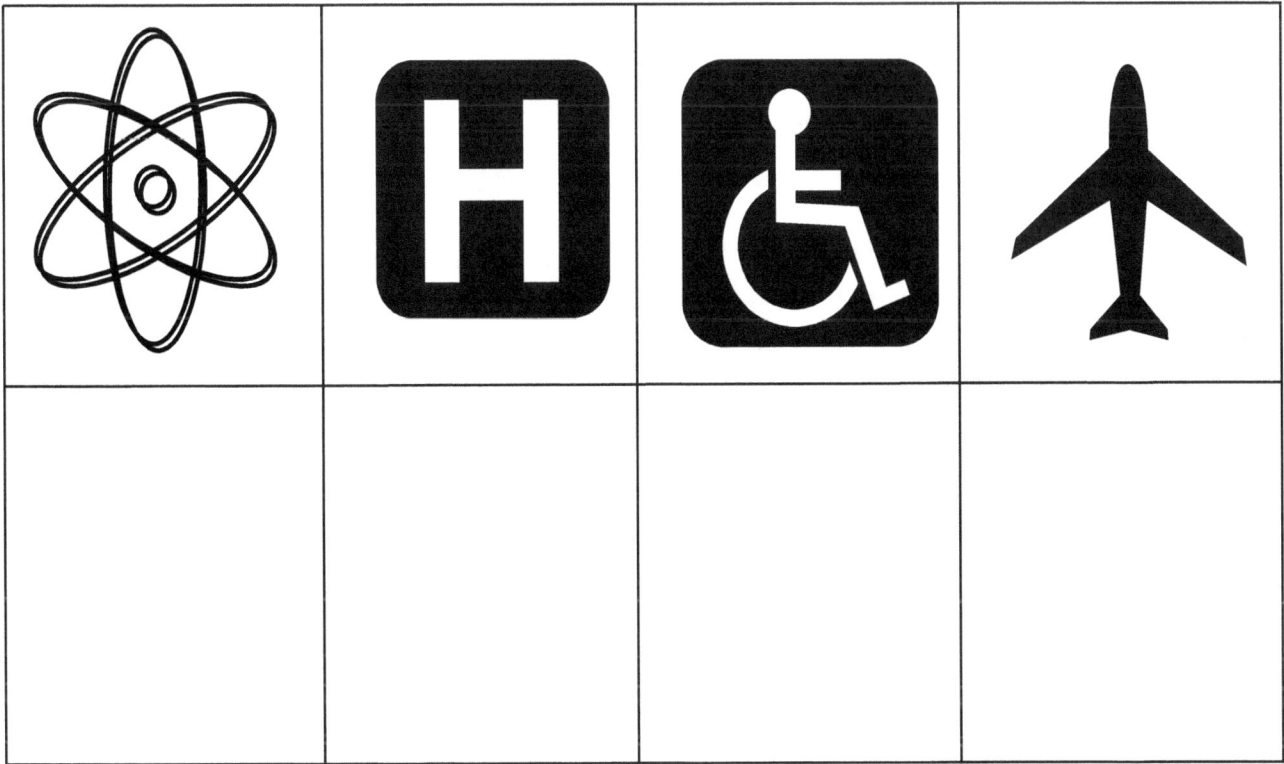

create your own symbols

love	strength	family	friends
seasons	snow	rain	sunset

art
starts
lettering

upper case calligraphy - practice your letters
using a pencil first

A *B* *C* *D*

E *F* *G* *H* *I*

J *K* *L* *M*

N *O* *P* *Q*

R *S* *T* *U* *V*

W *X* *Y* *Z*

lower case calligraphy - practice your letters using a pencil first

a b c d

e f g h i

j k l m

n o p q r

s t u v

w x y z

write these words & numbers in calligraphy

apple

football

1 2 3 4 5 6 7 8 9

calligraphy practice paper

bubble letters

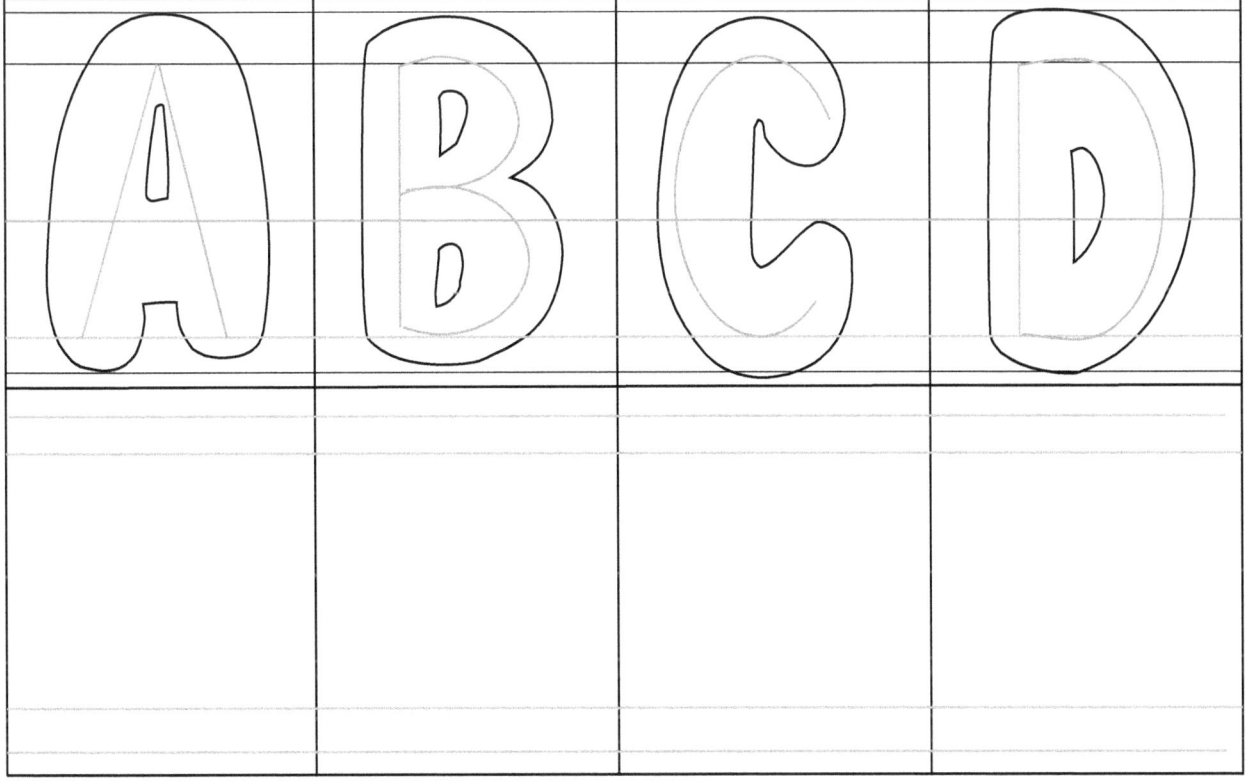

bubble letters

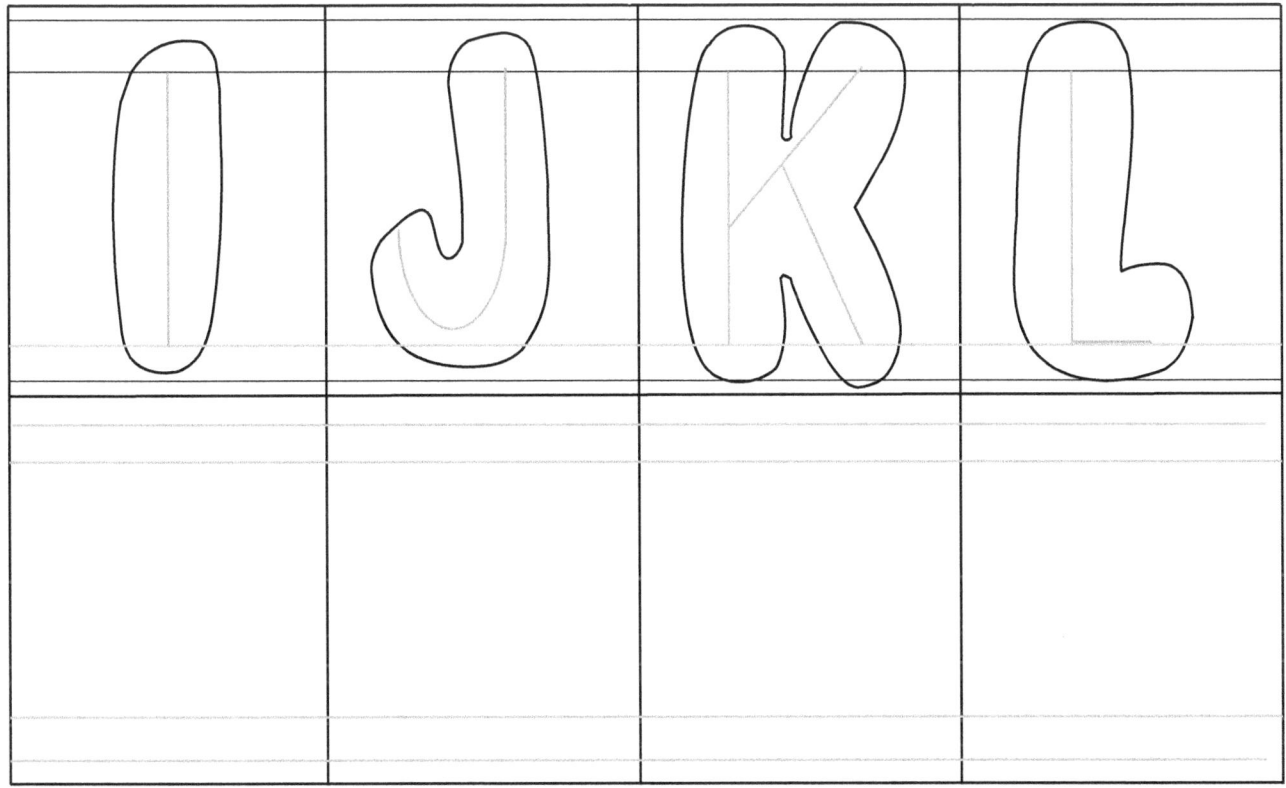

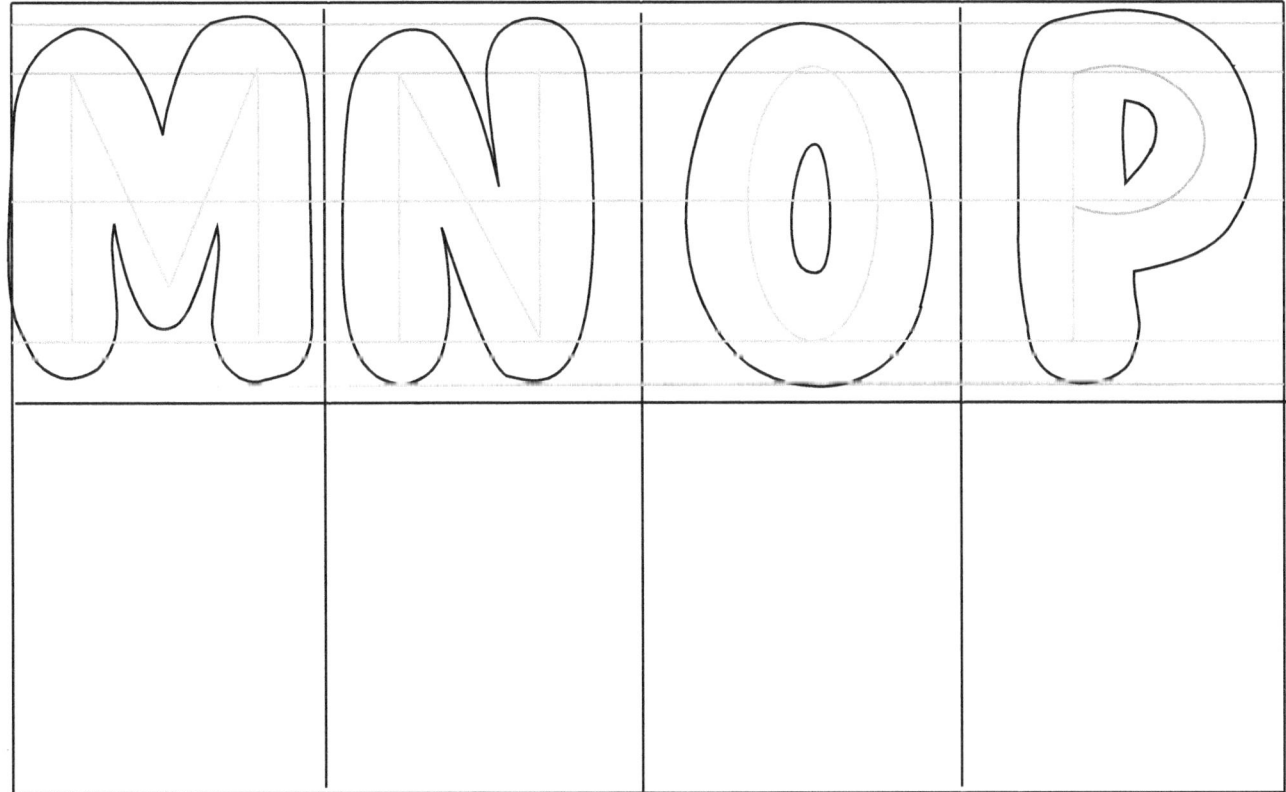

bubble letters

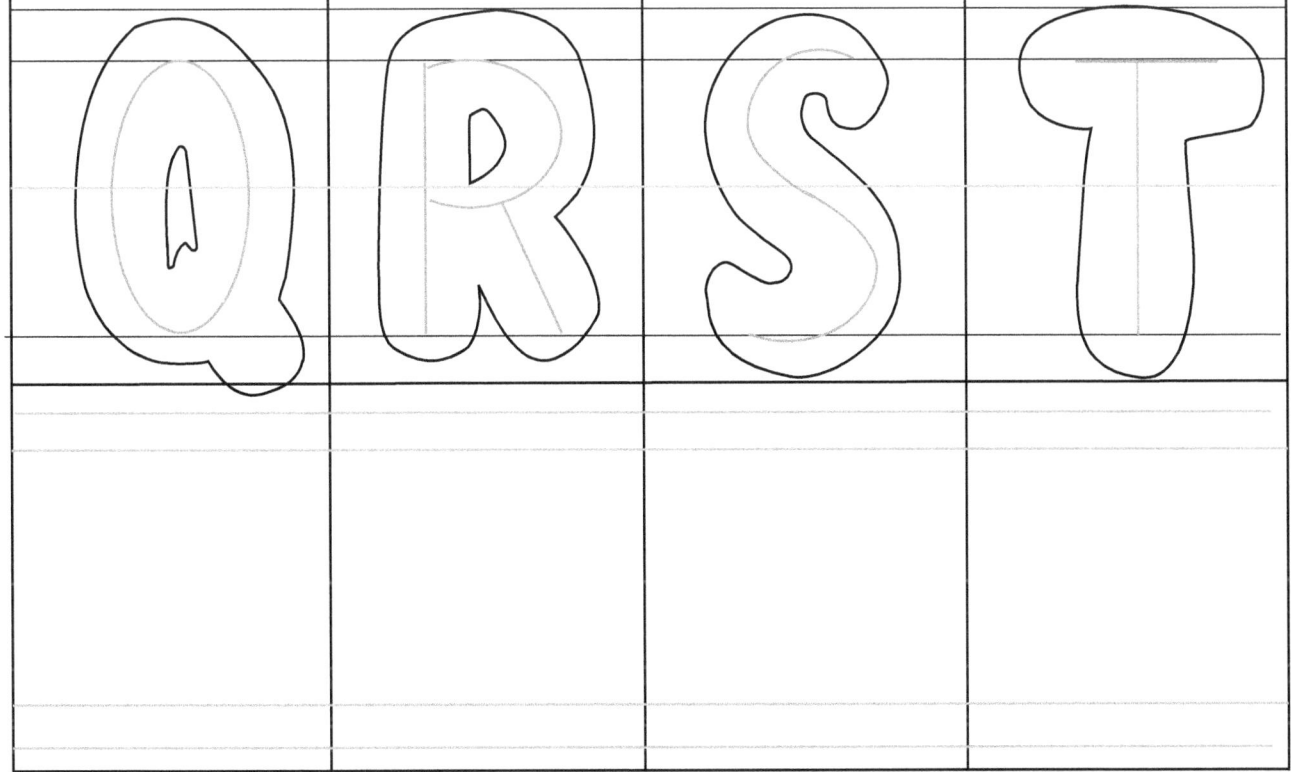

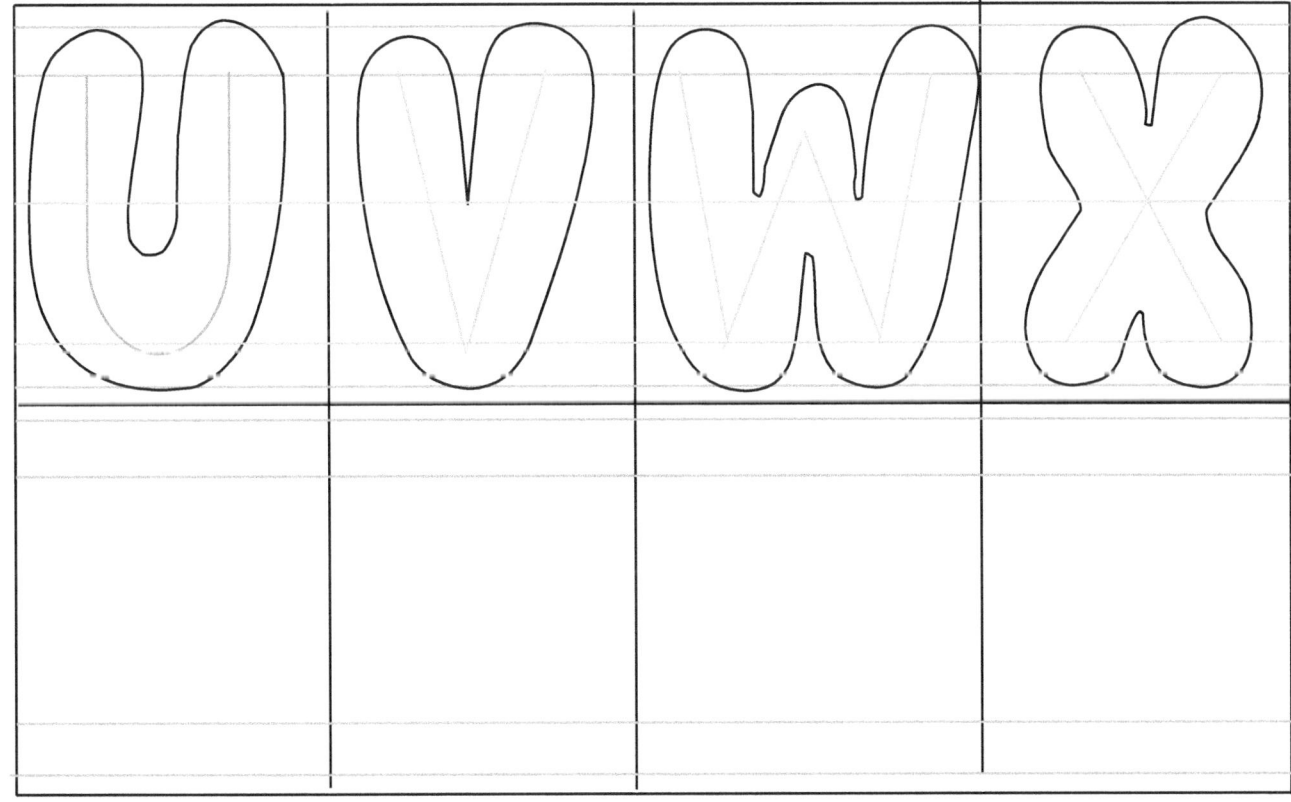

bubble letters

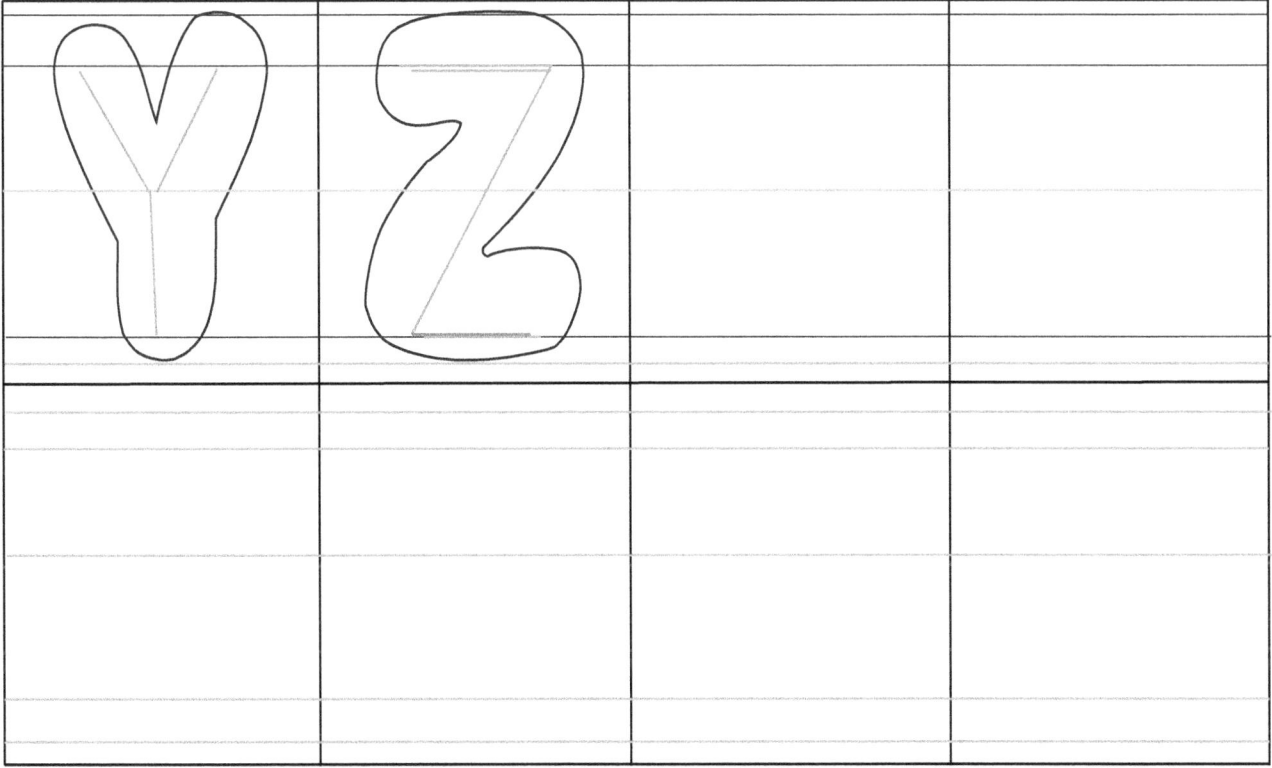

bubble letters practice

art
starts

art appreciation

famous pop artists

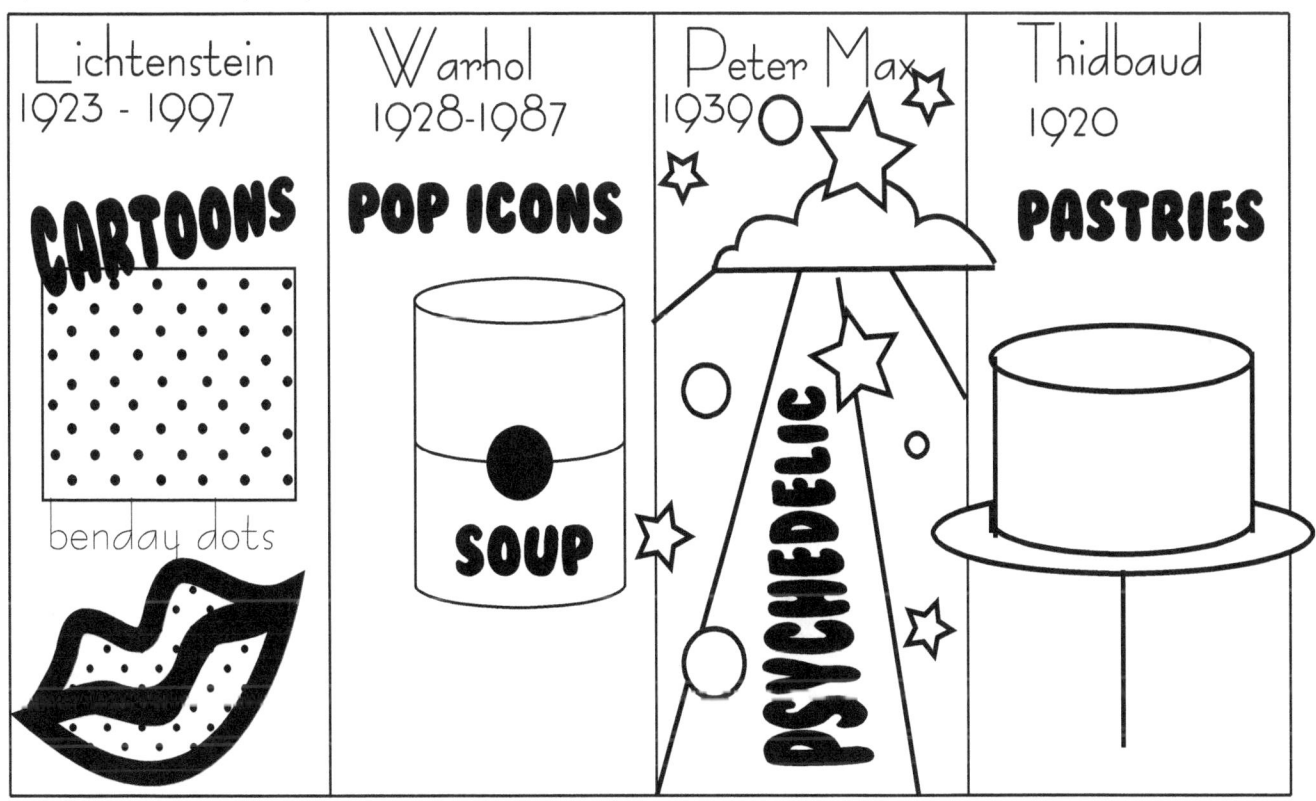

Lichtenstein
1923 - 1997

CARTOONS

benday dots

Warhol
1928-1987

POP ICONS

SOUP

Peter Max
1939

PSYCHEDELIC

Thidbaud
1920

PASTRIES

recreate the above information on these 4 pop artists

some famous pop icons

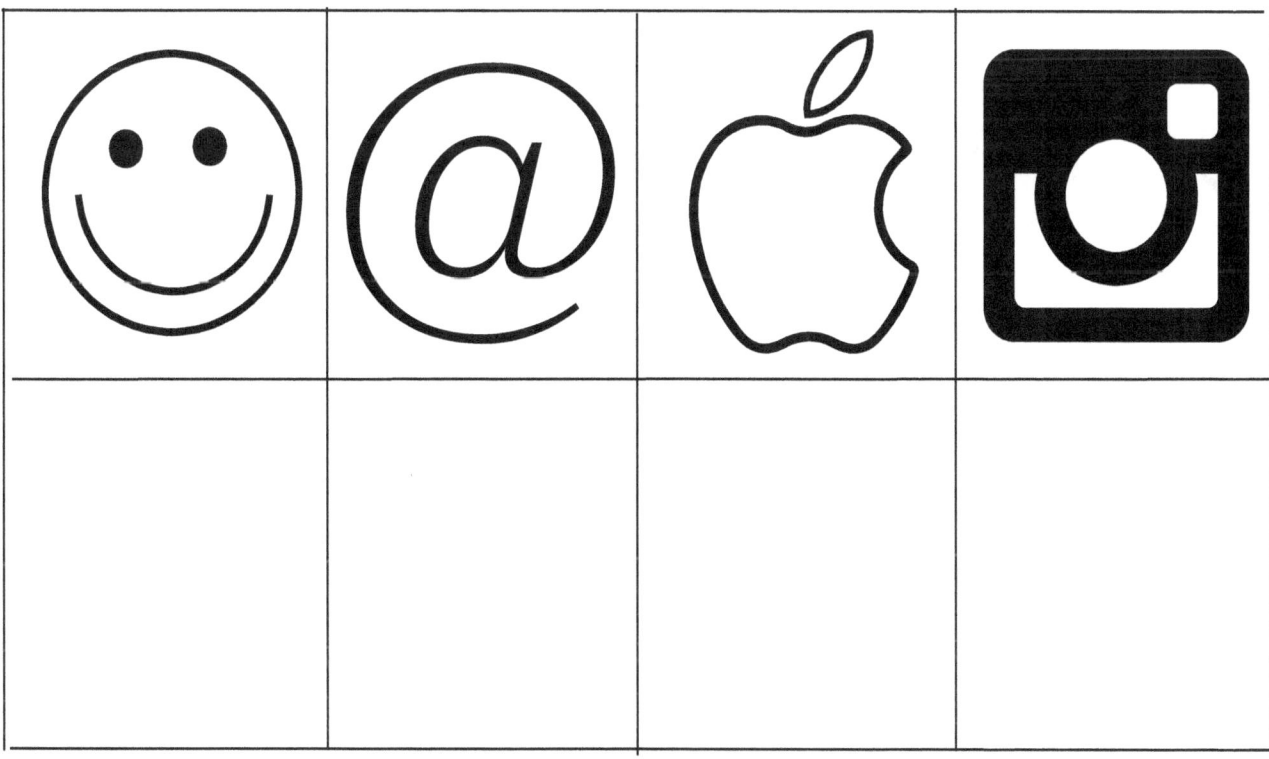

research and draw eight pop icons

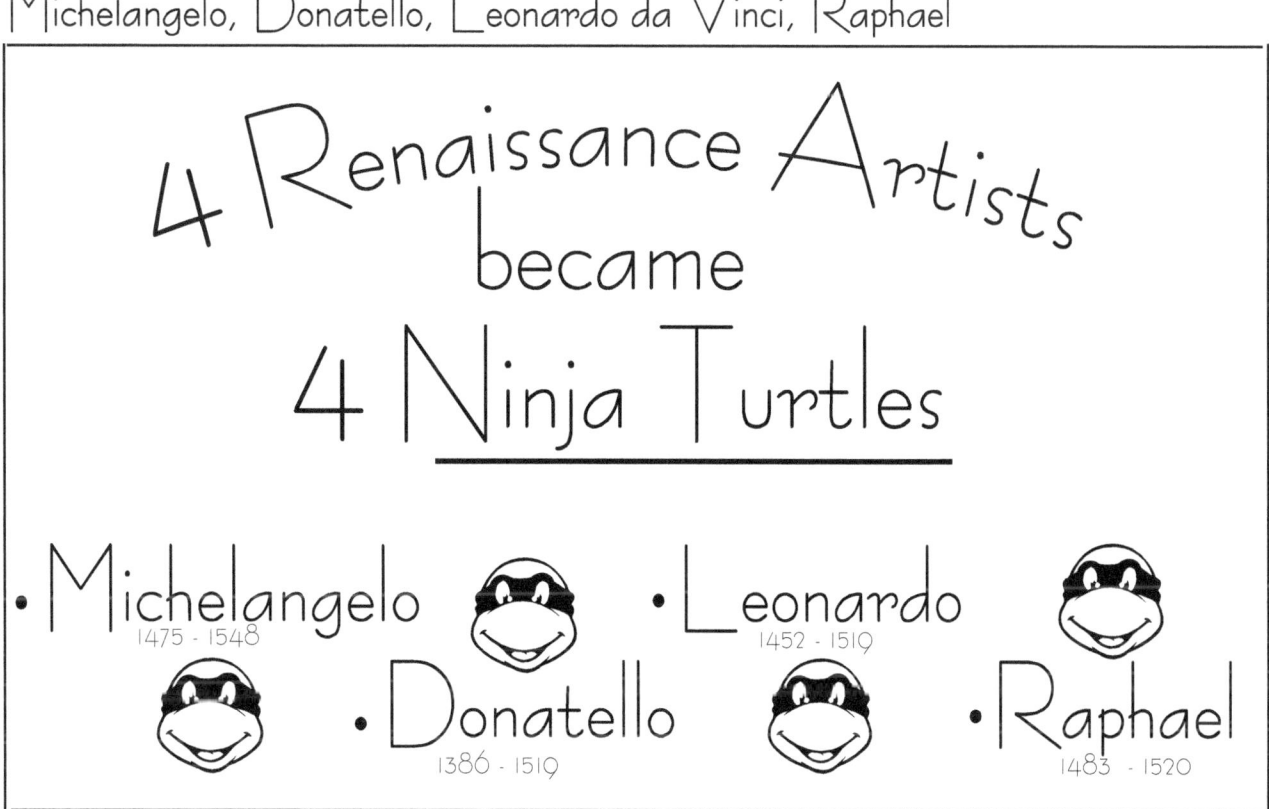

4 Renaissance Artists became

4 Ninja Turtles

• Michelangelo
1475 - 1548

• Leonardo
1452 - 1519

• Donatello
1386 - 1519

• Raphael
1483 - 1520

Which artist did which works of art?			
Sistine Modonna The School of Athens	Mona Lisa The Last Supper	Bronze David Mary Magdalene	Statue of David Ceiling of Sistine Chapel
_____	_____	_____	_____

Which country were these artists from? _____	What is Leonardo's whole name? _____	Why do you think the Ninja Turtles were named after these artists?

Pablo Picasso

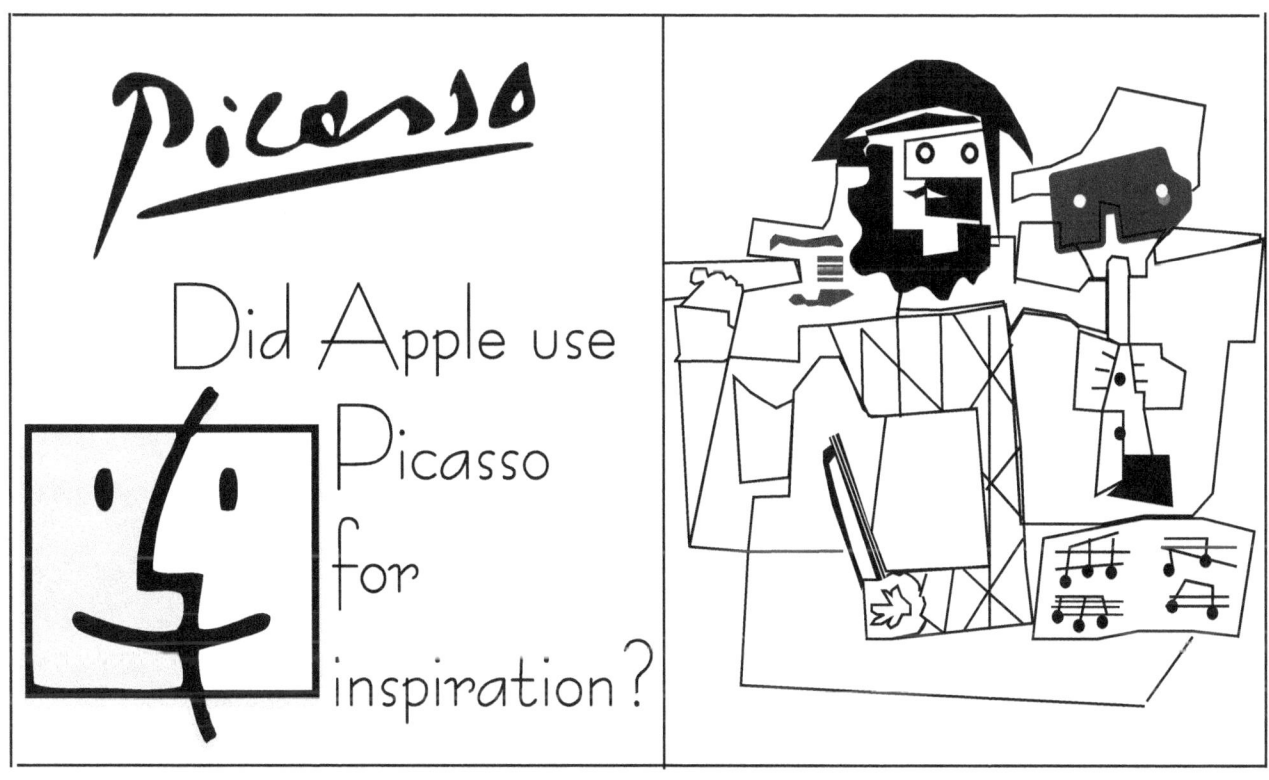

Did Apple use Picasso for inspiration?

When did Picasso live? _____	Above is a portion of a Picasso painting - what is the titile of the painting? _____	What year was this painting done? _____	Draw a simple Picasso style object.
What is another painting that you enjoy by Picasso? _____	Picasso had several "periods" of art during his life - name two: _____	"Bread and Fruit Dish on a Table" (1909) is from what Picasso style? _____	

Henri Matisse

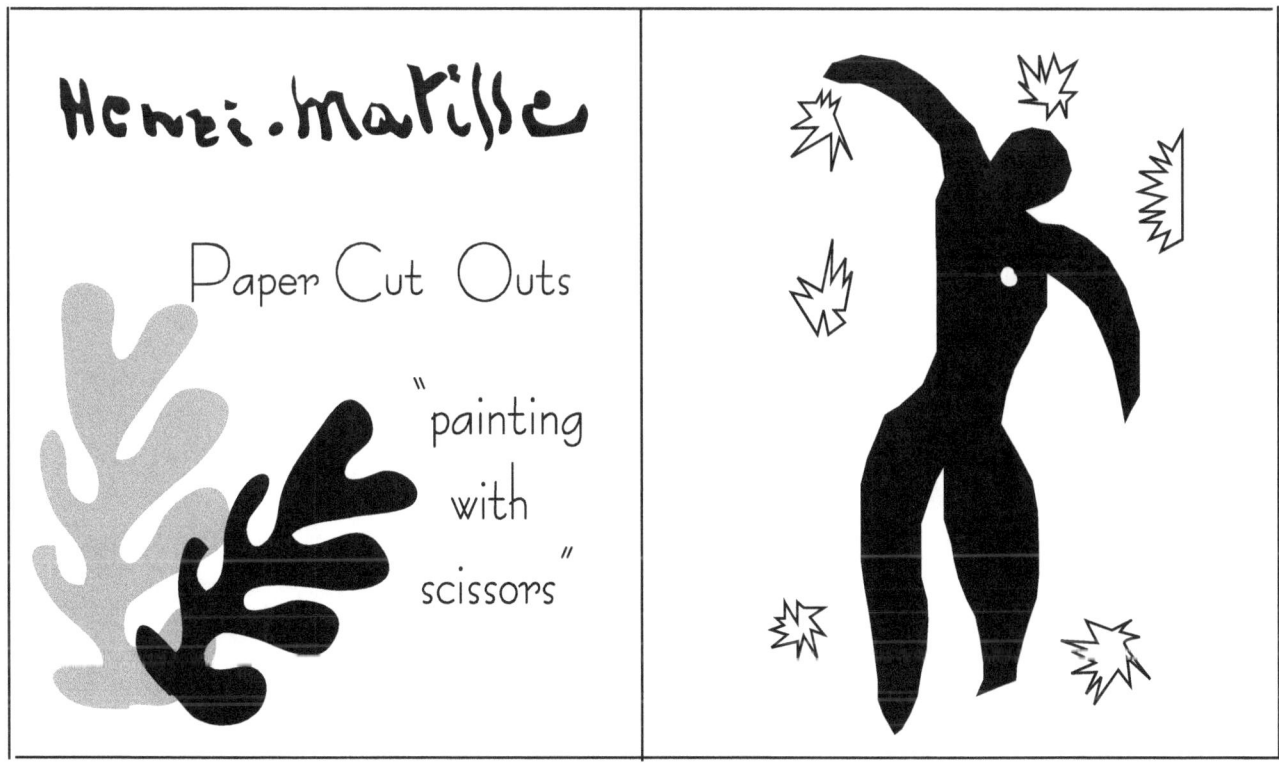

Paper Cut Outs

"painting with scissors"

When did Matisse live?	Above is a tracing of a Matisse cutout. What is the title of this work?	Cut out at least three paper cut outs in the style of Matisse and paste here. ⟶	
_____	_____		
Matisse also did paintings. Name a painting that Matisse did.	Why did Matisse end his life doing cut outs? _____ _____		
_____			

art starts

sketchbook prompts

sketchbook prompt

flames

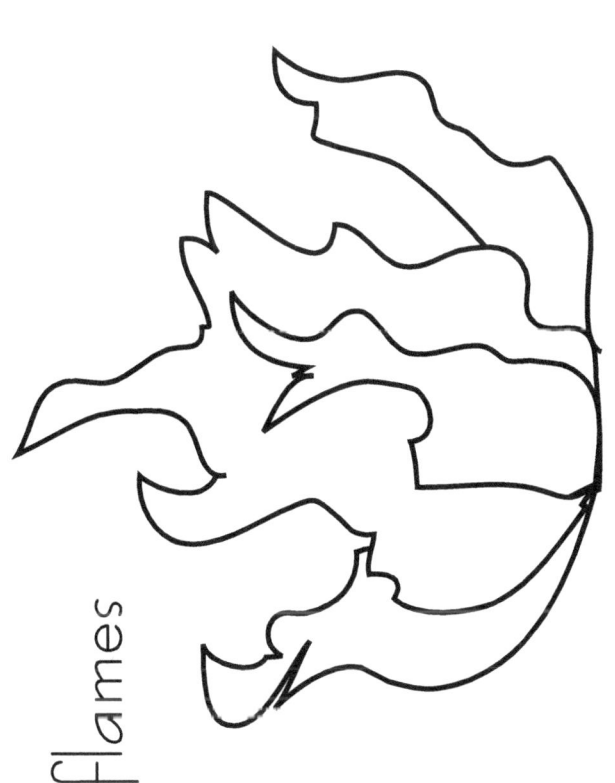

Draw a flame that covers your entire page. Using color pencils, color in the flames showing shading and blending of colors. Do not color in "coloring book style" where colors show no variation. Keep your coloring smooth and color in the direction that the flame burns.

sketchbook prompt

strange news

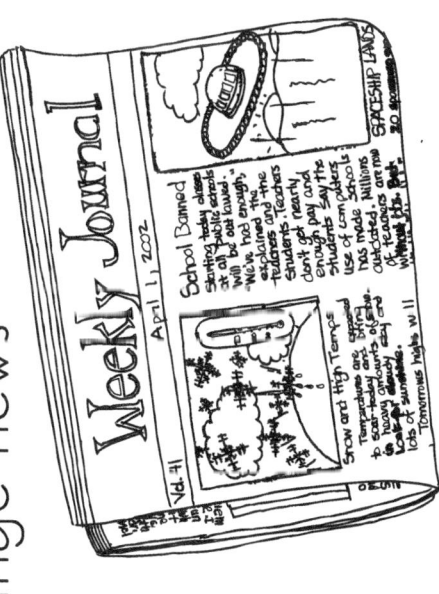

Draw the front page of a daily newspaper that is published on April 1 - April Fool's day. Your front page should have some difficult to believe headlines and a picture or two. Make sure you outline with a black sharpie and use a couple of different values of gray.

Draw an Insect

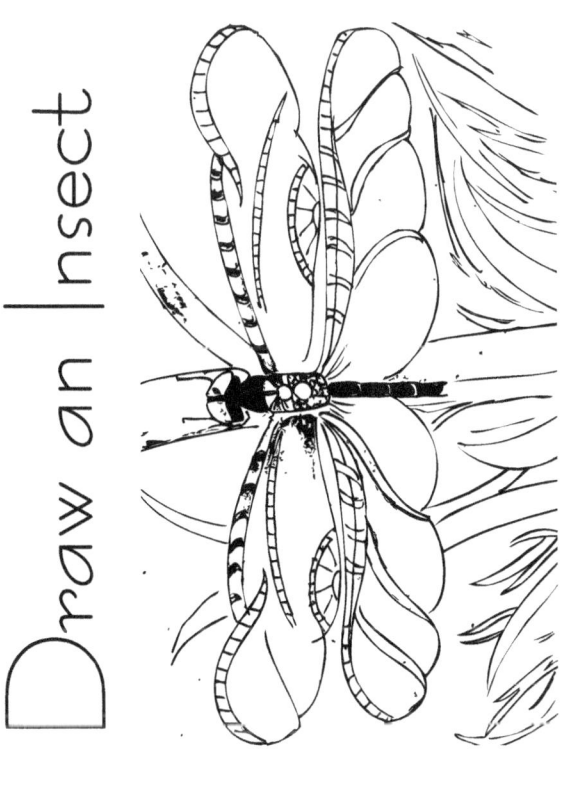

Look through your science book or online to see photographs of insects. When you find an insect that you like, draw it by giving it your own style. Afterwards, outline with a sharpie and add color.

Draw a Tree

first the trunk and branches......

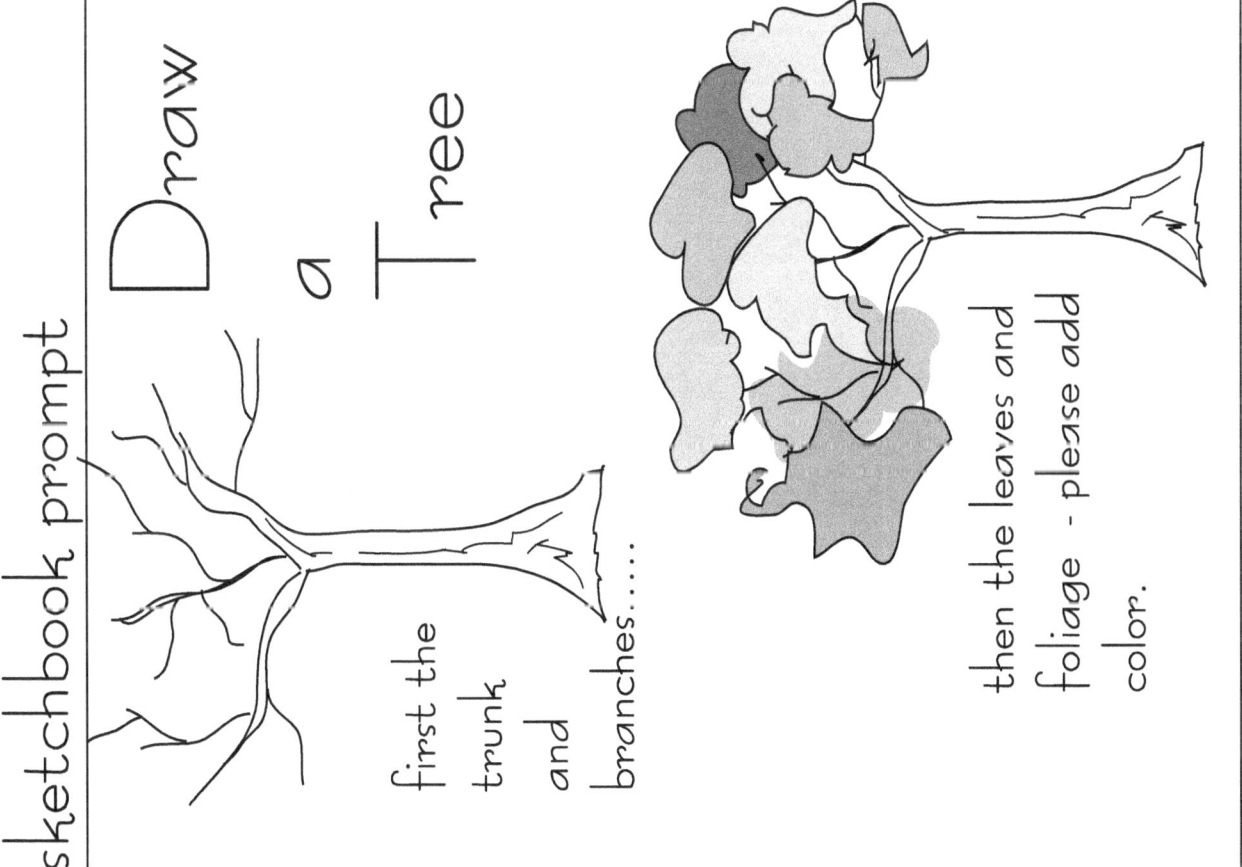

then the leaves and foliage - please add color.

sketchbook prompt

Going in circles.......

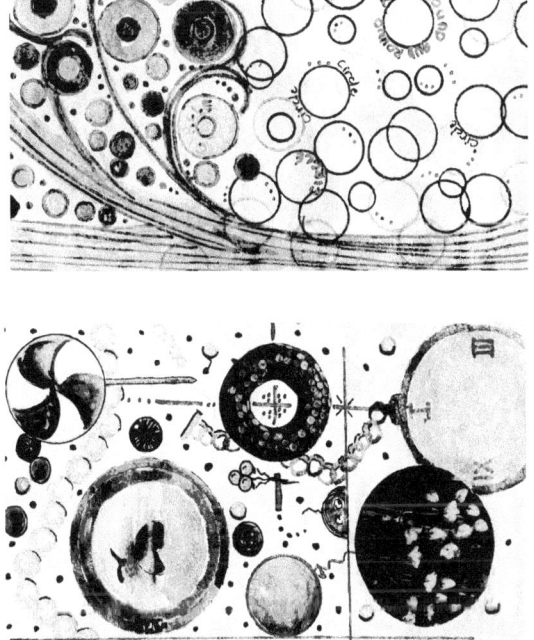

Circles are used in every kind of design from science to technology and especially in art.

Create a design that uses circles. Show a variety in your circles in the size, the medium you use, open and solid and thick & thin lines.

---

sketchbook prompt

Illustrate One of These Sayings

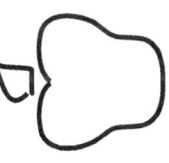

"An Apple a Day, Keeps the Doctor Away"

"Red sky in the morning sailors take warning, Red sky at night sailor's delight"

"A rolling stone gathers no moss"

Think about what you might do to illustrate. Although these are traditional sayings you can give them a modern twist.

An illustration is a form of art that brings an idea to life and tells a story. It is different from fine art that is just "art for the sake of art." Illustrations are found in books and magazines.

sketchbook prompt

make a pattern

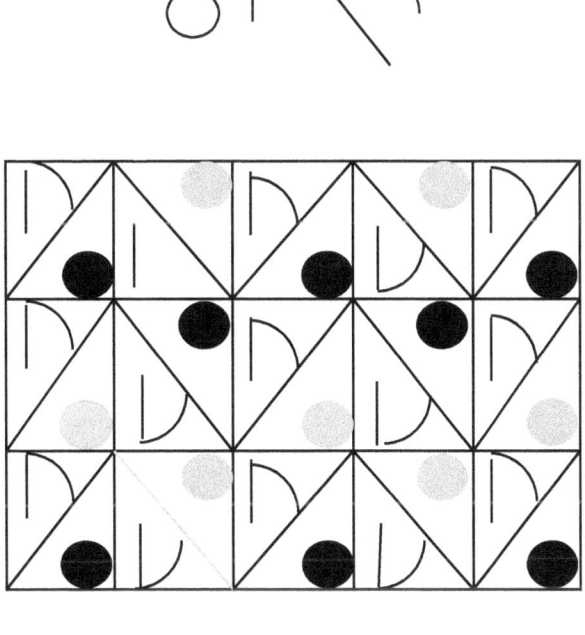

Divide your sketchbook page into equal spaces. Using a variety of at least four lines and shapes, make a pattern that covers the page. Color in your pattern while keeping in mind that your color makes a pattern also.

sketchbook prompt

it's a wrap

Find the wrapper from your favorite candy or other snack to replicate in your sketch book. The drawing should look as much like the wrapper as possible. Look for the fine detail in the design and try to copy it as closely as possible. Bringing out the actual details and color will make your drawing pop. You should make the drawing larger than the life to make use of the whole sketchbook page. When you finish outline in black sharpie and color with color pencils.

sketchbook prompt

flower power

Travel back to the sixties when flower power was all the rage. Cover the entire page of your sketchbook with flowers. Then fill them in with color (your choice of medium), texture or crosshatching and lines.

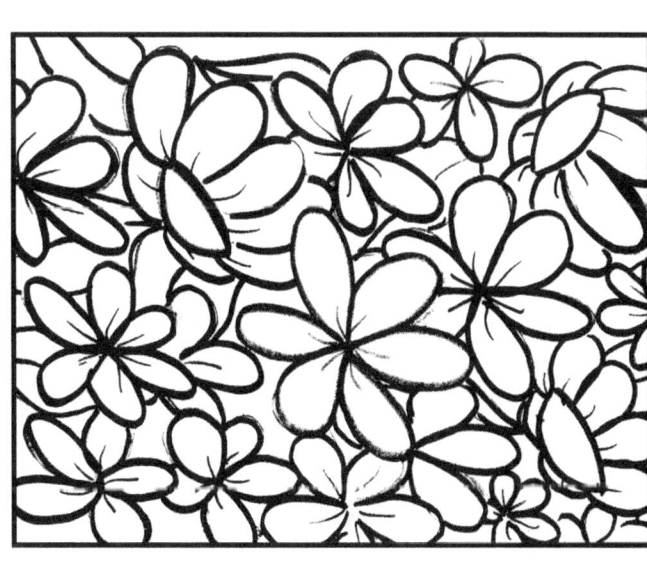

sketchbook prompt

jar of jam

Fill a jar with the "jam" of your choice. Some suggestions: musical jam, sports jam, shopping jam, traffic jam - you get the idea.

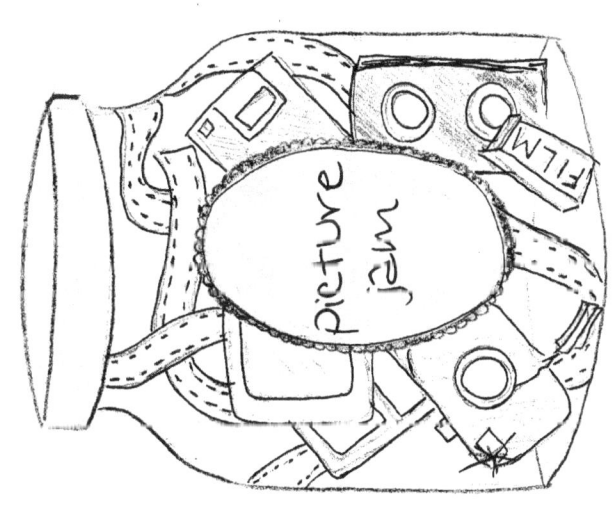

Outline your finished drawing with sharpie or color in your choice of medium.

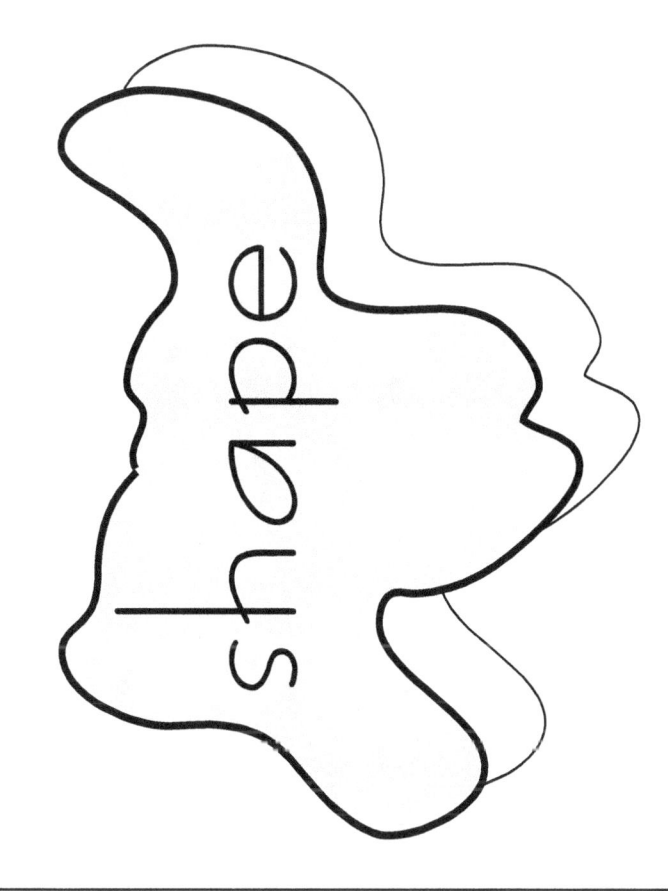

shape

Draw a shape and cut it out to use for a template for your drawing. Draw the shape you have selected repeatedly over the sketchbook page. Let the shapes overlap and run off the edge. Fill your shapes with color & texture. Where your shapes overlap let the color and the texture merge.

---

space

do you take up space?
do you live in space?
what is positive space?
what is negative space?

In your sketchbook draw four sketches showing space.

Each drawing must show:

-overlapping
-fore, middle & back grounds
-close objects larger
-distant objects smaller
-close objects rear bottom of drawing
-distant objects moving up the page
-bright/darker colors on near objects
-dull/lighter colors on distant objects

art
starts

graphic organizers

3 kinds of line

2 variations of lines

1 simple drawing using lines

---

3 things I learned this week

2 things I'd like to try again

1 thing that I enjoyed this week

Left panel

3 kinds of shapes

2 uses of shape

1 simple drawing using shapes

Right panel

3 ways to show space

2 uses of 1-point perspective

1 simple drawing showing space

artist research

art movement or style _____

2 interesting facts _____

_____

artist _____

_____

2 famous works _____

_____

shape vs form

draw one shape · one

draw two forms · Two

Three

draw three shapes and forms together

a little color theory

Fill in this chart using color pencil, no words.

A Hue

Its tint

Its shade

Its Opposite

Three of its analogous colors

element review

fill with texture

fill with lines

fill with shapes

show space

art
starts

early finishers

Salvador Dali

Salvador Dali is known for his bizarre painting style with clocks that seemed to be melting and animals that changed from one species into another. He was a part of the surrealist movement. Look up some of his works on the internet.

Using a sheet of white drawing paper draw something that you find bizarre. It can be an object, a landscape or a person. After you finish your drawing add color with your choice of media.

On the back of your drawing write one paragraph telling three interesting facts about Salvador Dali or about his art work. You will notice that Dali's apperance went along with his style of painting.

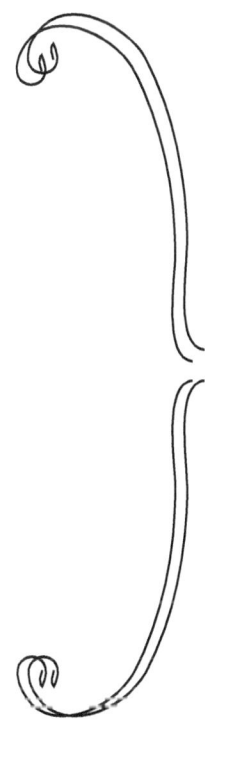

Piet Mondrian

Piet Mondrian was a member of the De Stijl art movement.

Go to a computer and look up "Piet" Mondrian. You will notice that he has a very distinctive style to his paintings. You are going to create a painting based on the concept of his style.

You will use a 12" x 16" piece of tag board or something similar,

You will be using a large sharpie and watercolor.

Be creative but try to stay true to the style of "Piet"

When finished with the painting, on the back write a short paragraph telling three interesting facts about Mondrian or his art work.

Have Fun!!

van gogh

One of van Gogh's most famous paintings is "Starry Night." He was a post-Impressionist painter who painted in bright colors and small brush strokes. Using tempera or acrylic paint, create your own starry night or sunny day painting. Remember to use small brush strokes in a swirling, circular pattern to mimic the painting style of van Gogh.

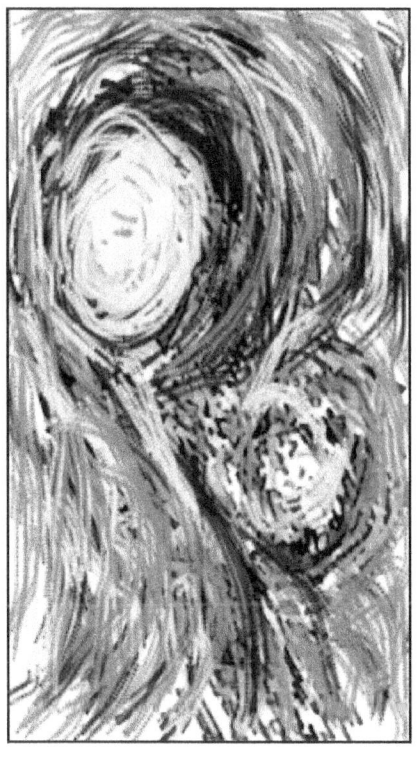

georgia o'keeffe

Georgia O'Keeffe was best known for her large, close up paintings of flowers. Using a 9 x 12 inch sheet of watercolor paper, draw your favorite flower very large so that the edges run off the page. After you have finished your drawing use watercolor to bring it to life, Georgia O'Keeffe style.

alice neel

Alice Neel was a famous portrait artist. She had a unique style and could capture an individual's personality in her work. Research some of her art work and draw a portrait of some ore you know or someone famous.

You may use pencil shading or water-color wash to add value and color.

alexander calder

Alexander Calder is most well known for his amazing mobiles. But, he also worked in other media too. In fact he made a small scale circus, Cirque Calder, with working parts. It was portable and Calder traveled around the world giving performances of his miniature circus. However, Calder also worked in paint and printmaking, and his paintings had the same movement that his mobiles had. Research some of Calder's paintings and try your hand at creating a painting that shows movement.

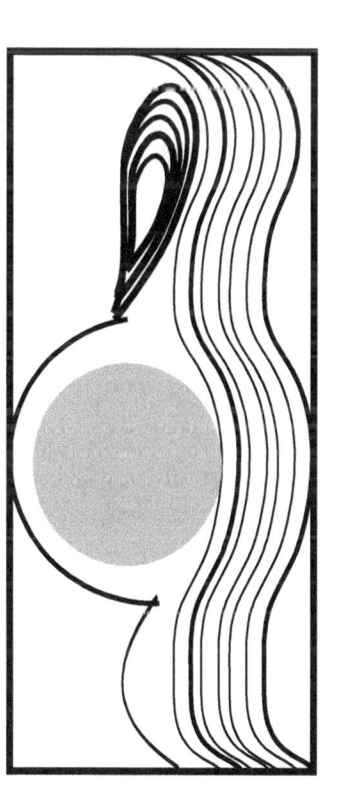

peter max

Peter Max is known for his Pop Art work in graphic art and illustration. He used psychedelic images and bright colors in designs that were different and exciting. Colorful stars, sun rays, peace signs, and animated people galore run through the art work of Peter Max.

On a 9 x 12 inch piece of drawing paper try your hand at a little psychedelic art.

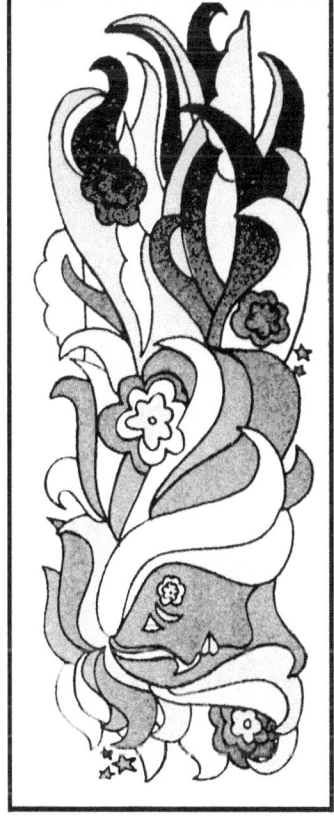

andy warhol

Andy Warhol was a member of the Pop Art movement in America in the 1960s. He is probably best known for his "Campbell's Soup Cans." Pop Art is short for Popular Art and in the 60s, with the invention of pre-made food for the first time, soup in a can was popular.

Using a 9 x 9 inch piece of drawing paper, divide it into even sized sections. In each section repeat a pop icon.

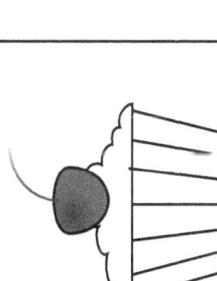

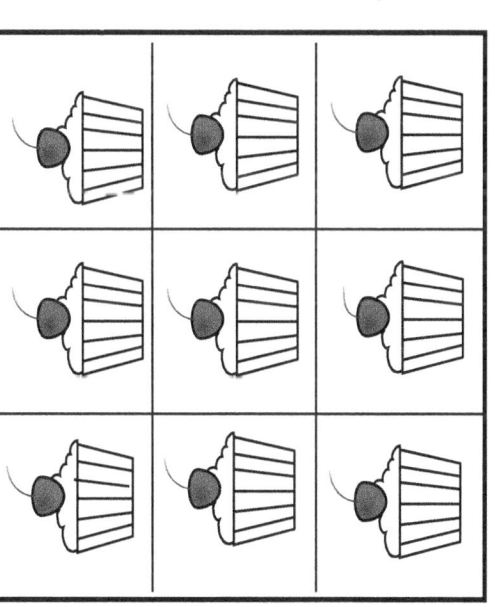

more fun

Using a sharpie, fill in each line with a pattern. A pattern sheet is attached or make your own.

pattern fun

Using a sharpie fill each square with a pattern. A pattern sheet is attached or you can make your own.

patterns

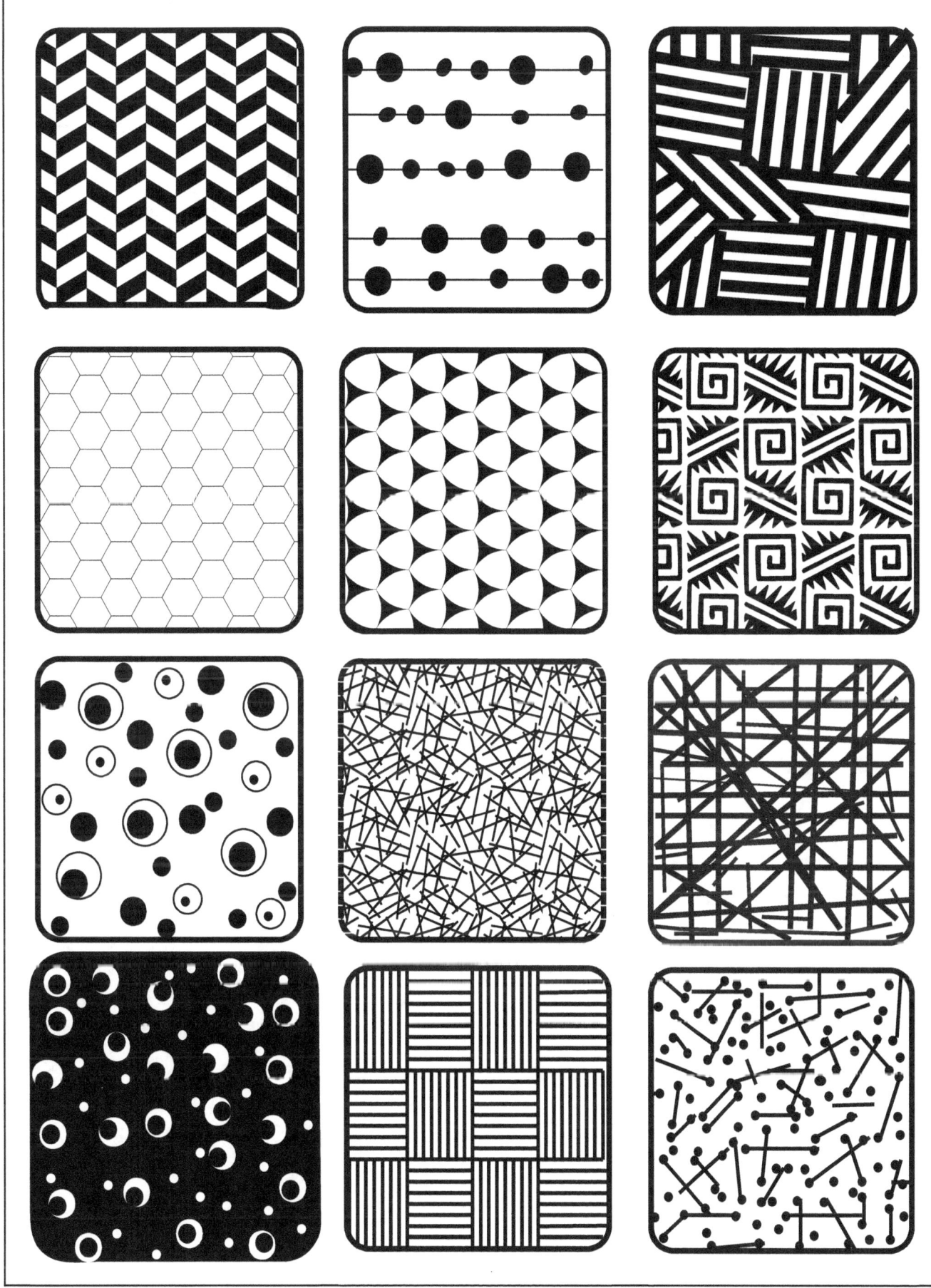